Books by Ernst Jünger in
The Eridanos Library:

Aladdin's Problem, translated by Joachim Neugroschel

A Dangerous Encounter, translated by Hilary Barr

Eumeswil, translated by Joachim Neugroschel

Julien Hervier

THE DETAILS OF TIME

Conversations with
Ernst Jünger

Translated by Joachim Neugroschel

MARSILIO PUBLISHERS
New York

Original French title:
Entretiens avec Ernst Jünger

Copyright © 1986 by Editions Gallimard, Paris

Translation copyright © 1990 by Joachim Neugroschel

Of this edition copyright © 1995 by
Marsilio Publishers
853 Broadway
New York, NY 10003

Distributed in the U.S.A. by
Consortium Book Sales and Distribution
1045 Westgate Drive
Saint Paul, MN 55114

ISBN 0-941419-95-9

All photographs are taken from
Ernst Jünger: Leben und Werk in Bildern und Texten,
Stuttgart, Klett-Cotta, 1988.

Printed in Italy

CONTENTS

PREFACE

These conversations are essentially the fruit of my meetings with Ernst Jünger on the occasion of his ninetieth birthday. After earlier interviews, which were published in French newspapers, he suggested that I act as his interlocutor for various German radio and television broadcasts connected with the celebration of his birthday.

Our conversations took place in German, at his home in Wilflingen, where the Great Foresters of the Stauffenberg family used to live, and which all fans of Jünger are well acquainted with. For me, our conversations remain inseparable from a luminous atmosphere that fused with either a sunny view of the dazzlingly snowy Swabian countryside or the warm intimacy of the forester's lodge, which is ruled with ardent discretion by Liselotte Jünger. Jünger and I would walk for several miles with the temperature twenty degrees below zero centigrade: our revivifying stroll was then followed by the sharp popping of champagne corks—an agreeable sound that often punctuated our conversations.

I myself translated them, adding a few notes that struck me as indispensable for mostly non-German readers. As for my questions, I have not hesitated to abridge them occasionally, since I am persuaded that the reader would rightfully prefer to hear Jünger's answers.

TRANSLATOR'S NOTE: The English translation is based on the French text, since the original German text is no longer extant.

I

THE AGE OF THE PATRIARCHS

Psalms. Lichtenberg.
The melody of life.
Decisive turning points.
Privileged Moments.

JULIEN HERVIER: I first met you about ten years ago, and you're still the same. You don't seem to have changed at all, it's as if you had discovered a real fountain of youth.

ERNST JÜNGER: I wouldn't go as far as that. Being ninety years old doesn't appear to be at all unusual. I still haven't noticed anything special about it. However, for the past year or so, I've been receiving very enjoyable mail, and whenever I run into anyone on the street, he instantly starts talking about my age. For me, this is a surprising event: life passes very quickly, and in Psalms, we are told that grass grows in the morning, and that it's already mown by night. Sometimes life strikes me as a lengthening day. I am often surprised to find this in my readings. In fact, I enjoy learning good things about the Germans: that's why I'm so interested in history. I spend part of each night reading history books, and recently I stumbled on old Emperor Franz-Joseph of Austria. For me, he has always embodied the typical and exemplary image of a very old man. And all at once, damn it, I realized that I was actually older than he: I must have truly reached a very advanced age! That was the kind of surprise I was alluding to. One doesn't always notice it so clearly oneself. I'm thinking of the prince regent of Bavaria. Once, at the age of eighty, when he was hunting, he said to his gamekeeper: "Here we are, hunting chamois as usual, and I don't notice anything special." And his gamekeeper replied: "Yes, Your Highness, but you can believe me, other people do notice it!" I also remember old Lichtenberg: he tells a story about a carpenter friend, whom he had first met in Göttingen thirty-seven years earlier: "That man doesn't look any older than he did when I first made his acquaintance. Yet he must have aged!"

The same is true for me, here in Wilflingen. I've known some of the farmers since they were boys, but they have scarcely aged in my eyes. On the other hand, once you're at a certain distance, you notice it quite clearly in people whom you sporadically run into throughout twenty or thirty years, like TV weathermen with their frogs, telling you the weather. You notice that they grow older and you draw your own conclusions. And, like Lichtenberg, one can say in regard to growing old that you have to avoid overstretching your hopes and your legs.

HERVIER: When you celebrated your eightieth birthday, you wrote that reaching such an age was certainly no merit, but that, in any case, it constituted an achievement.

JÜNGER: That's right! And now that I'm about to hit ninety, I could repeat that same statement even more forcefully. Especially in our time: you can already see it in friends, in contemporaries who take their leave of you. First, your brothers and sisters, then your schoolmates, and then the buddies from your regiment, those from the First World War and those from the Second. It all makes you very very uneasy.

HERVIER: Isn't that the saddest experience: when you remain as vital as ever and you see so many friends and near and dear passing away?

JÜNGER: Yes, it's a lament that goes back to the most ancient times. Goethe too said that this progressive solitude was awful.

HERVIER: At the moment, do you think mainly of the past or of the future? Or do you live essentially in the present?

JÜNGER: The instant is preferable, the instant is everything, the instant is divided between the past and the future, and if you develop this idea with logical rigor, everything must be present in the instant. You only have to feel it as such. The classic authors always said: "If you spend something in an instant, eternity cannot bring it back to you." And other maxims of that nature. The decision is up to you. You can do stupid things that can never be made good again. On the other hand, you can have a fortunate encounter, that will change your life forever.

HERVIER: Today, when you think about your childhood and adolescence, does your life seem unified or more like a sequence of very different episodes?

JÜNGER: Our century has been full of twists and turns: if a man's life shows an overall unity, this is due to his character. You can be thrown into the most diverse situations. Yet what we might call the "melody of life" has been there from the very outset. And until the ship goes down, we keep playing the very same tune, as they did on the Titanic. This may be true of every life, but not all the melodies are charming.

HERVIER: If you had to point out the great caesuras of your life, what events would you call to mind?

JÜNGER: That is a question that can be answered in so many different ways. First at all, life is a river, isn't it, and this river has a certain constancy to it. That is to say: I remain constant, while events change. If you want to talk about caesuras, you have to consider both the historical caesuras and the personal caesuras. I'm thinking, for example, of the first amorous adventure, which, naturally, constitutes an important cut, opening a new universe. Then there are biological caesuras—that is: a person is a child, an adolescent, an adult, an old man, and finally a patriarch. When I congratulated my friend Carl Schmitt on his ninetieth birthday and paid him a small compliment, he answered: "Old age is over for me. I am now entering the age of the patriarchs." Those are the biological caesuras. And the historical caesuras in a life such as mine, which has been going on for nearly a century, are also very sharp. I was born in the nineteenth century, and in a way, I still feel its imprint even though I experienced only five years of that century. On this point, I would like to quote Talleyrand, who said that if you didn't live in the eighteenth century, then you don't know what living is! The nineteenth century did not have such a definite character in regard to the nature of society; yet it still remains to be discovered. One day, when I was strolling with Valeriu Marc, an old Jewish friend, who has worked on Lenin, he said to me: "After the nineteenth century, people will lick their fingers at the very thought of it!" And today, when we've entered periods of turbulence, we can only second that statement, at least if you come, as I do, from the upper middle class, which felt in utter harmony with the scientific and social conceptions that were current in those days.

Naturally, my parents also had certain revolutionary tendencies. My mother, who came from Munich, found a lot of elements that interested her in *Jugendstil*. The French call that style *fin de siècle*—and I myself was very interested in the ideas of that *fin de siècle*. You've read my story *A Dangerous Encounter* in which the *Jugendstil* decadence plays a major part. The story takes place at a time when, I believe, the Eiffel Tower was half completed, and the Dreyfus Affair was in the making. Concerning my forecast for the twentieth century, I have two special frames of reference. The technological one is the sinking of the Titanic—it is not an excellent forecast. And the social frame of reference is the Dreyfus Affair. This constituted the victory of democracy over the reactionary forces, one might say, even if this term is not entirely apt. The Dreyfus Affair plays a great part in my childhood memories. My father often talked about the *petit bleu*. And I was just a little older in 1911, when the Titanic went down. It is such frames of references that count in our lives. I'm speaking about purely historical events. I remember the day—I'm not sure what year it was—when Halley's Comet appeared. In any case, I was fourteen or fifteen years old. My father was there, and he was showing us the comet, which was not very big, but which we could distinguish very clearly—like a huge bean, if I may say so. And our father declared: "Among all of you, Wolfgang may be the one who gets to see it again." I believe it's supposed to return next year or the year after that. In his rationalism, my father had made a prophecy based on probabilities. However, the reckoning of probabilities was deceptive. My brother Wolfgang was the first to die: it was the youngest who left first. It was as if my parents had conferred a special strength upon the firstborn children: my four brothers and sisters actually died in the reverse order of their births. But aside from the events that touch history, like the appearance of the comet, there are inner explosions that offer completely unforeseeable surprises. However, I have managed to preserve my style, even in wars.

HERVIER: Of all your experiences, which ones have counted the most for you?

JÜNGER: There are experiences that are a pure addition of exterior events, and there are experiences that concern the inner man, and these are probably the strongest. For me, a major event was the great offensive of March 21, 1918. This experience was so powerful that I transposed it in terms of the Icelandic sagas. It was a great encounter: thousands of men perished within minutes. This dying was instantly communicated to the landscape, but it is difficult to describe such a phenomenon: for instance, fear is abolished. This is already a sign that enormous forces are very close. But we can also say that being in the jungles over Rio de Janeiro, on the outskirts of a glade (humming birds flit about, and you have the impression that the flowers are about to open) is also very beautiful. Or at any rate, this is beautiful, for war is not beautiful, it is only terrible.

HERVIER: And in the eighteen volumes of your complete works, which are your favorite books?

JÜNGER: I will only answer as follows: the important thing is to have worked on something radically different. That was what happened to me in regard to *On the Marble Cliffs*, where I had an impression of pure inspiration. It was apparently a situation that made the work directly necessary, guiding my pen. You probably also know a very short text of mine—what can I call it: is it an essay, is it a dream?—*Visit to Godenholm*, which has been read widely in both France and Germany, especially by young people, who have immediately responded to it. Around here, there are some Celtic fortifications: one of them is called the Heuneburg. Now, one evening, a female friend suggested that we go there. I objected: "It's late, the sun is already setting." But we went there all the same. We were on the battlements of those fortifications; and I had the impression that on that very day, something must have happened—it's what is known as "a day of destiny," the kind of day filled with a special meaning that affects events or will affect them some day. There was a very disquieting sense of something odd, as if liquid air were pouring upon that place, an air that was both icy and yet burning in a sense. It was a great moment, which concretized more or less during an instant.

HERVIER: At ninety years of age, a man could turn his back on the world. But instead, you are on a kind of peak, from which you contemplate everything with greater clarity and precision.

JÜNGER: One could certainly turn one's back on it, and this would be very agreeable. Schopenhauer was born under a similar constellation. But, after acting for a long time like a kind of sharpshooter, he became the object of more and more attention, which he gratefully accepted. As for me, it would be very pleasant devoting myself to my coleopterans. As Goethe said, one withdraws bit by bit from the world of appearance. . . .

II

THE WAR

The First World War.
Reading Sterne.
War and literature.
The Storms of Steel. Storm.
The Second World War.
Mobilization and forecasts.
De Gaulle and strategy.
The French Campaign. The occupation.
In Russia. Rommel. Defeat.

HERVIER: The First World War constituted one of your major experiences as a man and as a writer. What do you feel when you think about the young lieutenant that you used to be, covered with glory and wounds?

JÜNGER: My reaction is very complex. In any case, I would never say that I was completely wrong. Quite the opposite: a man has to be capable of respecting his own history. I genuinely like that young man, even though I feel very removed from him. During World War I, I reacted a lot more passionately, as did everyone else, in France and England too. All young men were prey to violent emotions. Why should anyone back away from it now at any price? Today, it would be dreadful to insist that that enthusiasm led to nothing. I'm perfectly aware of it, but I would still like to pat those young men on the back.

I became a nationalist purely under French influence, especially by reading Barrès right after World War I. Barrès was truly enthralling. He was the one who said: "Je ne suis pas national, je suis nationaliste [I am not national, I am a nationalist]." I instantly made those sentiments my own. Actually, what they did was to reactivate a great historical orientation—namely, the influence of the French Revolution on the German situation. The wars of liberation were made possible only by the phenomenon of Napoleon. The monarchies frowned on them. When Frederick William III watched the parade of the national guard, which was not part of the regular troops, he said, "That's the Revolution on the march!" They were singing, they were enthusiastic, he didn't much care for that. Wilhelm I, the first emperor of Germany, was extremely commonplace. One of his generals wore a shirt which had a bullet hole from the Battle of Sedan, and the Kaiser was offended, it was against the rules. These petty traits can make people very uncomfortable. When the emperor was riding his horse along Mars-la-Tour, he saw a Hussar corpse by the side of the road, whereupon he said: "His uniform is still in good shape, it ought to be laundered!" However, this does not mean that Wilhelm I was not a very good monarch. It's like chess: the king is the piece that moves least of all. Wilhelm II, by contrast, was far too mobile.

HERVIER: Do you sometimes dream about the war?

JÜNGER: Actually, I seldom dream about the war. It doesn't seem to have influenced me as deeply as literature. I've always read a lot, even during offensives. At the great offensive of 1918, the last one in which I participated, and in which I was seriously wounded, I had Lawrence Sterne's *Tristam Shandy* in my map case. On the one hand, I was engrossed in the tactical situation. I had invented—if I may say so— a certain form of progression, which consisted of attacking the different platoons successively, in waves. I watched the line of fire becoming visible in the heart of the landscape, and I was delighted to see how skillfully my men moved through the danger zone. At regular intervals, there were pauses lasting one or two hours, during which I read Sterne. Then the gunfire resumed, then I went back to Sterne. And, astonishingly enough, the book left a deeper mark in my memory then all the combat. In other words, literature is indeed more important for me than personal experience, no matter how concentrated. I was wounded during the offensive, and I continued reading at the military hospital. Today, I still like to read Sterne. In his way, he is a writer keeping a journal.

HERVIER: How did you begin writing yourself?

JÜNGER: It was never really my intention to write. Before the outbreak of World War I, I was planning to go to Africa. At that time, I was already something of what is known as a *non-conformiste*. That was why I had gone to join the Foreign Legion, but I was not really visualizing a war. Rather, I was thinking about adventures in

Africa. I had read a lot of travel books about Africa: Stanley, *The Dark Continent*, works of that sort. I pictured the landscape as very beautiful, it must have been hot all the time, very hot. And then there were the animals, the primitive life. . . . But it all turned out very differently.

HERVIER: And did you keep up your journal during the war?

JÜNGER: Yes, that was something I always tended to do. Incidentally, I feel that it really was a journal. My notebooks still exist. There are, I believe, fourteen volumes, consisting partly of small pocket-sized notebooks. In this sense, the work is the digest of a journal: it sticks very closely to the events.

There are many people who remained in that position of a World War I author and never left it. First I described the entire war in *The Storms of Steel*. Next, *Grove 125* covered only one month of it, and *Fire and Blood* only one day. A bit later, when I wrote a book of minute observations, which I titled *The Adventurous Heart*, my old friends and buddies said: "Look, he's becoming a man of letters!" They didn't care for that at all!

HERVIER: Weren't you induced to publish by your father, who was very glad to see you keeping your journal?

JÜNGER: That's right. He probably didn't think of it immediately, but then he told himself that it wouldn't be such a bad idea. He always gave very good advice; and he also got the book printed. The first edition was a vanity publication. I wanted to have as little to do as possible with publishers and everything concerning them—I've always avoided all that. I am not a member of any literary society, any club, etc., etc. All those things are extremely secondary.

HERVIER: How did you hit on the title of *The Storms of Steel*?

JÜNGER: First, I thought of calling the book *The Red and the Gray*, for just before the war, I had very enthusiastically read Stendhal's *The Red and the Black*. Perhaps I should have kept that title, for those were the colors of the war that ignored the glittering uniforms. But by now, I was reading the Icelanders, and when I found the phrase "the Storms of Steel" in a poem, I liked it very much. Today, I feel somewhat different about it.

HERVIER: Aside from your journals, you also wrote a short and fragmentary war novel, *Storm*, which you have completely forgotten.

JÜNGER: Completely. It was published in a newspaper in Hanover. At that time, I had so many personal problems that one can understand why I stopped thinking about the novel. It was rediscovered by my friend Hans-Peter des Coudres, the great specialist in the bibliography of my works. *Storm* was reprinted as a small book and also in my *Complete Works*.

HERVIER: This novel offers a very different testimony to the war than your other writings do.

JÜNGER: I haven't even glanced at it. What's it like?

HERVIER: It reveals more of a bourgeois mentality, and the aesthetic element, with a hint of decadence, is highly present in the young men who talk about war.

JÜNGER: Oh, that's right! They're talking in a shelter. As I've told you, I'd forgotten all about it.

HERVIER: Do you ever reread your own works?

JÜNGER: Generally not. Once I've written a book, it's sort of like a snake skin that I've sloughed off. I go back to it only because I have to revise it. Meanwhile, two complete editions of my works have come out in Germany, and I had to do some revisions. For me, these texts are becoming more and more historical—that's the most pleasant thing to be said about them. And the same holds true for my readers. I was twenty-three when I finished *The Storms of Steel*. The book was constantly reprinted, it's been translated twice into French, and even after the last war, there have been three new editions in Germany, where it is now my most widely sold book, even more than *On the Marble Cliffs*. Of course, it's not read the way it was in 1920. It must have a very special effect, particularly on readers who did not experience the events, but who want to find out what happened back then. Where you're sitting right now, that's where the Argentine writer Borges sat, I believe in 1982. He visited me specifically as a reader of that book. The first [Spanish] translation was done around 1922, at the initiative of a group of Argentine military men. Borges had read it in his youth, and he said to me (we were speaking French): "Ce fut pour moi comme une explosion volcanique! [For me, it was like a volcanic eruption!]" I had never suspected that my book could exert such an impact; when I wrote it, I was merely rendering an account of my experiences. Something vaguely similar happened with *The Worker*. I've heard that *The Worker* is having quite a resonance in Italy. You can judge for yourself, since you participated in the colloquium that took place in Rome in 1983: they talked about *The Worker* quite a lot. There was a whole group of Italian Communists who found the book very enlightening. But for me, these problems have lost their urgency. I could draw a comparison to the laying of mines; thirty or forty years pass, and all at once, a mine that was buried a long time earlier goes off. I am now in very distant waters, and for me it's more a source of astonishment than joy.

HERVIER: You experienced the two wars in very different circumstances.

JÜNGER: Yes, I believe it was the same for all my contemporaries. As I told you, when World War I broke out, the young people were extraordinarily enthusiastic in our cities, just as in London, Paris, or Moscow—it was a kind of intoxication. Whereas when the hostilities broke out in 1939, everybody felt sad and dejected: "Do we have to go through it again! How stupid to repeat it!" Enthusiasm was out of the question.

I must admit that right before the declaration of war, I didn't really believe it would happen. A few weeks earlier, Ribbentrop had convened a meeting in Fuschel, where he resided in a confiscated castle: he called several people together, including Sieburg, myself, and a few others. He explained that he wanted to set up what is now called a "think tank." If one of us wanted to go on a mission to China, Russia, or anywhere else, he need only say the word. We could telephone him collect any time, day or night. In short, he was very obliging, and he then launched into a political survey. I thought to myself: "These people are bluffing, there's not going to be any war, the others will realize it." And it went on like that until the invasion of Poland.

HERVIER: You were mobilized on the spot?

JÜNGER: One morning, when I was reading Herodotus, I was informed that a telegram had arrived, and that I was to report to Celle. And that night, I still heard people saying that everything was going to work out. But in the morning, the domestic came into my room. I asked him: "How are things?" He replied: "Bad, very bad." I was then asked what I would like. Since I could hardly say that I wished to serve in a garrison, I asked to be sent to somewhere on the front lines to take command of a company.

HERVIER: What were your feelings at that time?

JÜNGER: At that moment, I felt that things would be taking a very bad turn. "Either there will be a revolution immediately"—and that was why I also packed a civilian suit in my officer's kit—"or else it will be a very long trench war, as in 1914-1918." In the mean time, I had written a tactical essay titled *Fire and Movement*, explaining that the machine, the engine, had introduced an entirely new element into warfare.

HERVIER: That essay is very close to the notions advocated by de Gaulle during that same period.

JÜNGER: Precisely. I must even admit that I was influenced by de Gaulle, who had worked on the idea of total warfare.

HERVIER: As you did in your essay on *Total Mobilization*.

JÜNGER: Yes. In fact, the whole story went as follows. Right after the war, I had expressed my views on "fire and mobility" in several discussions. The infantry inspector, a certain von Taysen, summoned me and ordered me to write new military instructions. He attached me to a commission at the War Ministry, on Friedrichstrasse, and we worked on platoons, squadrons, and companies. That was when I invented certain dispositions and certain movements concerning cordons of sharpshooters—the lines and groups of sharpshooters that were employed during World War II. And it was during that project that I consulted French military journals, in which a young officer named de Gaulle detailed his general ideas on these issues. I had almost forgotten all those publications in the *Militärwochenblatt* [*Military Weekly*], but recently a researcher in the military archives sent me those articles on infantry offensives, movement, etc.

HERVIER: In 1939-1940, you participated in the campaign on the French front.

JÜNGER: After the winter that we spent on the Western fortification line, during what was called the "phony war," a bunch of imbeciles wanted to take photos and, of course, got mowed down. I went after them, and for that I received another Iron Cross. It was very pleasant, getting it for that rescue operation.

Next, we moved forward, but I was never brought into action with my company; we ran behind Guderian's tanks. Our vanguard saw a little action, but very minimally. At that time, there was a kind of remission during the advance through France, with the success of the Blitzkrieg. I told myself that everything was going a lot better than I had thought. I imagined, just as certain Englishmen did on the other side, that we were coming to terms. We had captured some French officers, with whom I discussed matters: "You'll take Alsace, but you have to leave us Lorraine." As they filed past us, those endless columns of prisoners kept shouting: "Peace! Peace!" And I replied: "It will come, it will come—it's certain." They had only one desire: peace. But Churchill dashed their hopes completely. It was then that everything turned sour. I told myself that I had been right nevertheless: it had only been a remission, as in an illness.

Just between us, I was in favor of negotiating, it would have spared us millions of deaths. The world state progressed all the same, for all those national issues were already obsolete.

Next, Stülpnagel and Speidel summoned me to the general staff in Paris, which was a total surprise: I experienced the war in a very different way than I had envisioned.

HERVIER: Your position wasn't very easy, as a German officer in a country that you love.

JÜNGER: Well, of course, my material position wasn't bad. Contrary to other occupiers, I always tried to help out to the extent that I could, but there are many things I haven't mentioned, I don't want to flaunt my good actions. For example, one day, Colette came to see me, and she explained that she had a young Jewish friend who went out at night after curfew. He had been arrested, I think, or at least he was in hot water. I was able to give him a hand, it's the kind of thing that one enjoys doing and has the honor of doing. Gallimard also came to me for help—as you can read in Assouline's book about him, which has just come out. They wanted to send his son to forced labor in Germany—it was Claude, if I'm not mistaken. The goal of the operation was to put pressure on Gaston Gallimard. because he refused to publish some book or other that didn't appeal to him. All of a sudden, the German Institute or the embassy had sent Claude his marching orders. I told the story to Stülpnagel, who said: "That's unbelievable, it's out of the question!" And Gallimard remained very grateful to me.

HERVIER: You've written that it was particularly difficult helping the Jews.

JÜNGER: Yes, I talked about it in the afterward to my [German] translation of Léautaud's *In memoriam*. It was extremely difficult, as was shown by the case of the good pharmacist on Rue Lapérouse: he was always so obliging and helpful, and we all liked him. You went to the Gestapo people and told them this, and they replied: "Yet you know the Jews, you're telling us about a particular case and you're forgetting the context, the scientific aspect of the question,"—a Marxist would tell you the same thing—"you're ignoring the overall scheme, the general perspective. Otherwise you wouldn't come and bother us with this sort of individual case. We obviously could let him go, but that would constitute a complete infringement of the rules." That was the way they answered us. Which is what a Marxist would say about Afghanistan: "You haven't studied the problem. Even if this troubles you in a specific case, it is an integral part of the overall line."

HERVIER: In *Heliopolis*, the hero vigorously intervenes to help some Parsis, whose situation is similar to that of the Jews under Hitler.

JÜNGER: But his efforts cause him problems, and he has to hide the young Parsi woman. That was what my brothers did in Berlin, where they managed to hide some Jews, the Cohens, who proved very grateful after the war. That was also the attitude of Gerhard Loose, my translator and exegetist, who lives in New York and went to great pains for me.

HERVIER: You yourself were in great danger after the failed assassination attempt of July 20, 1944?

JÜNGER: At that time, I was, regrettably, forced to burn certain documents about that period. Stülpnagel had assigned me the task of recording with extreme precision the history of the increasingly tenser relations between the [Nazi] Party and the Wehrmacht. There would have been enough material to enthrall a Machiavelli. First of all, the relations with the Führer, which were of fundamental importance. And then the German police interventions in Paris, to which the commander-in-chief was, of course, very hostile. I also focused on the problem of hostages, assassinations, and reprisals. A few documents still exist, but, despite their historical interest, I don't think it would be opportune to make them public at this time.

To give you an example: a member of the German administration was strolling along the Champs-Elysées at nightfall. All at once, he was hit in the back of the neck and collapsed. It was the kind of affair that would have led to the execution of at least twenty people. But then it turned out that the man in question was an epileptic and that he had dreamed the whole story. Thank goodness the incident could be cleared up. That is the sort of anecdote that I recorded.

HERVIER: Nevertheless, certain French intellectuals still won't forgive you for being in Paris during the war, as we saw on the occasion of the tribute that was paid to you at the Centre Georges-Pompidou in January 1980.

JÜNGER: In the face of power, I know very precisely what I must do, I have to be cautious, I have to bend in such and such a way. There are forms, there are rules in regard to power, whereas things are very different when it comes to intellectual encounters, which are regulated by a kind of equality of rights. Once the element of freedom has a part to play, things turn complicated and become more difficult. That is plainly the advantage of strict order, of the Prussian Army, the Society of Jesus, or the British Navy. Everyone knows what he has to do. But if you enter a café frequented by *literati*—those people are a lot more perfidious than generals! One can even say that discipline ensures a certain form of protection for subordinates.

HERVIER: You left Paris for a while to go to the Russian front, during a period when you were thinking about the conditions under which Germany could obtain an honorable peace.

JÜNGER: I was sent to Russia once, to the Caucasus. It was a bit like Gogol's *Dead Souls*, I made the round of generals and collected their opinions. But they were in the thick of battle, their backs were against the wall, and they had no interest whatsoever in political problems. The young officers told me: "We don't agree with Hitler, but there are things one doesn't do. If we don't hold out here, then everything will be doomed." And they weren't wrong.

HERVIER: It was at that time that you conceived your book entitled *Peace*.

JÜNGER: In Paris, at that time, they were trying to find a political solution that would prevent the worst, especially in the East. These efforts were thwarted by the [Allied] demand for unconditional surrender. I studied the problem as a responsible man, and I asked myself what could be the terms of a peace that would lead to the formation of the Europe that everyone desires today; except that I was far more optimistic back then. However, *Peace* is, first of all, a book that I conceived for myself. I attempted to figure out the moves in advance, as in a game of chess, but I had no ulterior political motives when I was writing the book. However, I was friends with Speidel, and I showed it to him when he came back from Russia. He liked it so much that he instantly dispatched a motorcyclist to La Roche-Guyon, to take a copy to Rommel, who read it in one night and then said: "This is a text one can work with!"

HERVIER: Do you think that if it hadn't been for Rommel's death, history would have taken a different route?

JÜNGER: I believe in any case that Rommel was the only one who could have ended the war, the only one with enough prestige in the population. But as you know, he was wounded near Livarot shortly before the assassination attempt. And I still asked myself what would have happened if he hadn't died. Rommel felt a certain attachment to Hitler. He agreed about changing course, but he felt they had to convince the Führer. That was what he said in his telegram: "If the situation becomes untenable in military terms, then politically, we have to. . . ." And for that alone, Hitler bore him a terrible grudge.

Peace could also have had some dreadful consequences for me, but luckily, it never came up when Speidel was interrogated in Küstrin. After the war, I could find no publisher or printer for that little text. Typewritten copies were circulated in Paris; there was even a banned edition, which was seized.

HERVIER: Do you believe that the defeat of Germany was inevitable and necessary?

JÜNGER: Misfortune is necessary in order to allow change and the birth of the new. History is filled with overriding necessities. The historical necessity of the First World War was that it did away with monarchy. The monarchies vanished among both the winners and the losers. The inherent necessity of the Second World War was the elimination of national states. Now, there are only huge empires, such as Russia, America, China; such is the form that power assumes today.

This is a necessity—as bitter as it may appear to some people. I said so in *The Worker*, and I repeated it later. The only thing to survive is the mythical figure of the worker. It transcends defeats, civil wars, fire and blood, and is even strengthened by them.

We have to admit it, even if I don't have too much personal sympathy with this figure, who is a product of technology, and even if my taste runs more to the romantic deviation. But if you propose to describe a situation, you are duty-bound to stick to the facts, though without neglecting the relationship to transcendence.

1. The siblings Friedrich Georg, Johanna Hermine, Wolfgang, Ernst, and Hans Otto in 1912.

2. Ernst Jünger's mother, Lily (Karoline) *née* Lampl (1873-1950), who came from a French-Bavarian family.

3. Dr. Ernst Georg Jünger (1868-1943), Jünger's father, who worked as an assistant to the chemist Victor Meyer at Heidelberg University. Soon after the birth of Ernst, the family moved to Hannover, where Ernst Georg opened his own laboratory.

4. Ernst Jünger in the uniform of the Foreign Legion.

5. With a girlfiend in 1924.

6. Jünger in the trenches during World War I (1915).

5

6

1915
Zacharias Zwinger
im Schützengraben

7. Lieutenant Ernst Jünger. One of the few infantry lieutenants to receive Germany's highest military decoration the "Pour le Mérit," he had formerly received the First Class Iron Cross, the Hohenzoller Royal Knight Cross, and a gold medal for being wounded in action.

8. Frontispiece from the first edition of *Storms of Steel*.

9. Lieutenant Jünger with his company Commander riding in Eitdorf, in 1920.

11

10. Captain Jünger on horseback, leading his company during the French campaing in 1940.

11. Ernst Jünger in Überlinger in 1937.

12-13. Photographed by Florence Henri in Paris, in 1942.

14. With his sons Ernst (left) and Alexander, vacationing in the Kirchhoster Garden.

15. Jünger's son Ernst in 1944, the year he was killed on the Russian front.

16. With his cat Li-Ping in 1950.

14

15

17

18

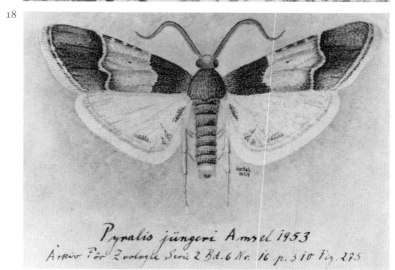

Pyralis jüngeri Amsel 1953
Arkiv För Zoologie Serie 2 Bd. 6 Nr. 16 p. 510 Fig. 275

17. Hunting for butterflies in Tuscany (Montecatini, 1950).

18. Pyralis Jüngeri Amsel (1953), a butterfly named by Jünger in honor of his friend Dr. Hans Georg Amsel, who in 1986 was awarded the first "Ernst Jünger Prize for Entomology."

19. With Albert Hoffmann (the discoverer of LSD), at his garden in Switzerland (1979).

20. With a Mantis Phyllocrania (1978).

21. Ernst and Liselotte Jünger with Jorge Luis Borges at their home in Wilflingen.

22. Ernst Jünger with president François Mitterand and chancellor Helmut Kohl during the German-French reconciliation ceremonies in Verdun, in September 1984.

III

CHILDHOOD AND ADOLESCENCE

African Games. The father.
A nineteenth-century rationalist.
Orphans and adopted children.
The mother. A sense of language and emotionality.
The second Westphalian view.
The mythical mother and dreams.
Hatred of school. Martin Buber.

HERVIER: What state of mind were you in when you wrote *African Games* and what is the relationship here between experience and the way it is shaped into a novel, or, as Goethe put it, between Poetry and Truth?

JÜNGER: I published this book in 1934, I believe. That was twenty years after my escapade in the Foreign Legion. But by then, I was already keeping a journal, which I was able to make use of later on. There were an amazing number of emotionally unstable men in Verdun, where the Foreign Legion had its recruitment office. And so some time ago, when I was given the honor of being received in Verdun, I was able to say in my brief speech that this city of Verdun was one of those that, like a few others, such as Paris and Laon, had a constant meaning in my life. I first visited Laon [Verdun] in 1913, going to the recruitment office of the Foreign Legion. Later on, in 1915, during the offensive launched against Verdun, I was wounded in *les grandes tranchées* [the great trenches]. And I returned a third time just recently, but this time as a friend. It's the most beautiful dream in the world: *la fortresse s'ouvre à l'ami* [the fortress opens up to the friend]!

But to get back to *African Games*: this was twenty years later, and I took my notes up again very precisely, even though I give the characters new names: for instance, Berger for the hero. The events are quite accurate, but they are transcribed into a more elaborate language.

HERVIER: Memories of youth likewise seem to play an important role in *The Slingshot* [*Die Zille*]. Are these still autobiographical elements, or is everything freely invented?

JÜNGER: My schoolwork was terrible, and so my parents sent me to Brunswick, to what was known as a "cramming school." These schools weren't run by the government, they were private, and the people in charge had rather brutal methods. They didn't spare the rod, and the students attending these schools were either too stupid or too lazy. However, my novel is not purely autobiographical. I might say that *African Games* was almost a portrait, while in the case of Clamor, the invented elements are more important.

HERVIER: Has your experience in the Foreign Legion played a certain part in your relationship with France?

JÜNGER: I couldn't say so. I had read Stanley and others, and I had always pictured the dark continent as a magnificent landscape. But all I found was sand and an unattractive military decor, so that I instantly fled. Meanwhile, my father intervened. All the documents are in the Foreign Affairs Bureau in Paris. My father moved heaven and earth for me. Just as I was about to run off a second time, I received a telegram: "The French government has granted your release; get your photograph taken!" That was the kind of thing my father always thought of. So I immediately went to a photographer, and the photo still exists. However, the experience per se was a disappointment, which, incidentally, has recurred. I spend my time chasing after landscapes that I know from books, and as a general rule, they've been so thoroughly spoiled by tourists that I no longer recognize my dream. So this story of the Foreign Legion is one of the great disappointments that keep recurring throughout history: each generation plunges into undertakings of that type, and this constitutes a not negligible part of literature. You always find that gap in Stendhal. He had a great image of Napoleon, while he himself had only an obscure job with his uncle Daru; while envisioning how wonderful it would be to be a cavalry officer—or how it might have been.

HERVIER: Your father's intervention was providential, for you had put yourself in an excessively difficult predicament.

JÜNGER: It's quite astonishing that I could have done that and subsequently become an officer. After World War I, everyone was authorized to consult my file. I read the recommendation of the highest regional officer. My father had lived more or less as an anarch: in any case, the officer wrote: "Dr. Jünger lives in comfort and pays no taxes. As for his son's joining the Foreign Legion—that has to be seen as a youthful folly." In the military, subordination was automatically punished with six weeks in prison. I was risking that kind of trial, which was being negotiated in Metz. But my father spent a tidy sum to hire an attorney named Grégoire, who played an important political role, and he managed to get the charges dismissed. If I had had to serve a prison sentence, I could never have become an officer.

HERVIER: Your father showed a lot of sangfroid and skill in ticklish circumstances. But what was your mother's reaction?

JÜNGER: My mother was more impulsive. Naturally, she was scared, while my father had already studied all aspects of the situation with logic. In case I failed to get out of the Legion, he told me: "They have a training program for junior officers. You have to take it!" He had already primed himself for all eventualities, while my mother absolutely wanted to have me back.

HERVIER: He seems to have had a very complex personality.

JÜNGER: The chemist in Turgeniev's *Fathers and Sons* greatly resembles him: a man of the French Enlightenment, who proceeds in a rigorously scientific manner, poking fun at the elders—that was how my father sneered at his parents. He had studied chemistry in Heidelberg and had been the assistant of Victor Meyer. We can certainly say that he lived as an anarch. Take this example out of a hundred: One day, my grandfather took my grandmother to a café outside the city so that she wouldn't make a scene, and he said to her: "Hermine, I have something unpleasant to tell you: our Ernst"—(that was my father)—"has gotten married, and he already has a little boy of four." You see, that was how he behaved.

HERVIER: In your *Journal*, you relate numerous dreams about your parents.

JÜNGER: In my dreams, I often encounter my grandmother, and she exerts a very powerful influence on this world of dreams. But my parents too have to be present frequently, perhaps even always. In some dreams, my grandparents are in front of a shop window, looking at the display. Someone is standing next to them, and they say something to him from time to time. After he's left, they suddenly realize it was my father or my mother. They must be so profoundly buried in the genes, that they are nearly identical with the person. Incidentally, there is something curious in regard to my grandmother and the places where we lived in Hanover, and most of which were destroyed, even though they survive in my dreams. Little by little, everything blurs more and more, as if a form of survival in dreams were dissipating, like a meteor, which leaves a trail of sparks that fade bit by bit.

HERVIER: Do you feel that you were influenced by your father's powerful personality?

JÜNGER: I regard what a father says at meals as more important than all schooling: in a way, my interest in history and my value judgments come from him. My father was a typical representative of the nineteenth century in that he appreciated great figures. It began with Achilles, continued with Alexander the Great, and went all the way to the Conquistadors and Napoleon. He was an outstanding connoisseur of the literature about Napoleon. And no lunch or dinner went by without my father's talking in detail about those subjects. In his youth, he had experienced the Bismarck era. He wanted to study chemistry. In those days, the study of chemistry was still a kind of adventure, and so my grandfather told him: "As far as I'm concerned, you're free to study chemistry at Heidelberg, but on condition that you also study something practical. You have to pass pharmaceutical examinations so that you at least have something solid to fall back on." And that was what my father did. Indeed, my grandfather's advice proved excellent, for my father began at the laboratory of food products in Hanover, which didn't work out at all. But then, with the money that was left over, he bought a pharmacy in Schwarzenberg, and it prospered. After World War I, we had the great inflation. I can still see my father on his threshold, crackling a wad of hundred-mark bills in his hands and saying: "This isn't worth much." And he quickly used it to buy a second pharmacy. Thus, my grandfather's advice got him out of two predicaments.

HERVIER: So what you especially recall about your father is his scientific and rationalist spirit?

JÜNGER: My father said: "I don't believe in eternal life, but I believe that one continues living in one's children." I, for my part, believe in a survival. As for children, one encounters such examples that I prefer the customs of the caesars, who were in the habit of adopting children.

HERVIER: In your novels, your heroes are frequently orphans, or at least without parents. As for the hero of *Eumeswil*, he despises his father. Could you explain this trait, or doesn't it have any special meaning in your eyes?

JÜNGER: It certainly does have a meaning. This hatred or at least— for that would be overstating it—this antagonism toward the father is well-known under the name of Oedipus complex, etc. If you wish to isolate a hero, it's an excellent way to immediately give him a certain distance. The hero of *Eumeswil* is essentially gifted in observation and history, to which he has devoted himself in the past. Consequently, it is good that he himself has no serious attachments. The more self-sufficient he is, the more freely he moves and the more acutely he can observe. Perhaps that's one of the reasons why the father was discarded or else counted as an adversary.

HERVIER: Clamor, the hero of *The Slingshot*, is also an orphan, and he is eventually adopted by one of his teachers.

JÜNGER: Yes, Clamor, who already bears a strange name. That was the name of one of my ancestors. In Latin, *clamor* means "clamor."

HERVIER: You've said relatively little about your mother.

JÜNGER: Yes, you'll probably find more about her in my brother Friedrich Georg's book. However, one doesn't talk either about the fact that one breathes or that the heart beats. This is an area that largely escapes literary investigation.

HERVIER: If you nevertheless had to pinpoint what you owe to your mother, what particular traits would you highlight?

JÜNGER: No matter what nation you belong to, it is always important to have parents who speak their language well. Language is virtually the most precious possession that parents can leave to their children. No matter how far the spirit of egalitarianism may go, the instant a person starts talking, you promptly know whom you're dealing with. And if you have a literary background, then with the first two or three authors a person mentions, you already know whether the dialogue is worth continuing, whether it has any chance of being fruitful.

My mother spoke a remarkable German, and she had a deep rapport with literature. She was a passionate reader, and madly in love with Goethe and Schiller. Before we learned how to read, she would frequently read aloud to us. I remember that she read Schiller's *The Bell* to us, and when she came to the verses, "Alas! It is the beloved wife. / Alas! It is the devoted mother," she would burst into tears. She was extremely impulsive.

She became more and more passionate about Goethe, and no year went by without her traveling to Weimar. She would take us along, giving us a chance to make the acquaintance of the sublime places of German Classicism. Thus we lived at The Elephant and visited Goethe's home and his country retreat. That's a very lovely memory. As a result, I owe a great deal to my mother as well as my father. Incidentally, I consider gratitude an essential feeling. In religion, too, I regard it as quite superior to a prayer asking for a favor. For example, I was struck by the fact that the Lord's Prayer expresses little gratitude, but formulates all sorts of requests. Thank goodness that hymns reestablish some sort of equilibrium. There is a whole branch of "hymns of praise and actions of grace," in which the Germans have excelled, especially during the Baroque period in Silesia.

HERVIER: In opposition to your father's scientific and rational character, I would be tempted to highlight your mother's literary and intuitive aspects.

JÜNGER: I probably owe a great deal to the Westphalian origins of one branch of my family. They had a great influence on me. There are some traits that can be transmitted only through women, for example certain types of color blindness. This illness only affects men, but it is passed on by women. I have certain ways of grasping things, something I really owe to my forebears in Westphalia. For instance, I've often told this story about my great-grandmother. One day, when she was a little girl, she was standing outside the front door (it was in Bramsche, I think), in Westphalia, and she saw a funeral procession pass by. A coffin containing a child was being taken to the cemetery. From where she was standing, she could see the cemetery gate. Terrified, she dashed indoors to tell her father—my great-great-grandfather—that a child whose name she knew was being buried. He asked her if she had really seen the burial. And when she said yes, he told her by way of reassurance: "You see, you dreamed all that. The proof is that this gate of the cemetery hasn't been used for a hundred years: everyone goes in through the large gate." But that night, there was a terrible storm, and the large gate collapsed, so that the coffins had to be carried in through the small gate. That story is part of the chronicle of my family, the Determanns, my Westphalian ancestors.

Those phenomena are frequent in Westphalia. The poet Annette von Droste-Hülshoff was very interested in them. She is very precise in her descriptions of people who are gifted with second sight in our area, in the countryside. I have to admit that in *On the Marble Cliffs*, more than one trait comes from there. After the 20th of July, I was stunned to see that I had pre-described the events very accurately.

Prince Sunmyura is none other than Stauffenberg. He fails in his undertaking, but the mere attempt is already very fine.

Getting back to my great-grandmother's gifts, those are phenomena that recall breathing or heartbeat, they concern a sphere that has nothing personal about it. That ancestress occupies a far more important place in the work of my brother Friedrich Georg than in my work. As for my grandmother, I dreamed about her for years—strange dreams that I gathered in a small collection entitled *In the Houses of the Dead*.

HERVIER: In your *Journal*, especially in the sections about World War II, there are dreams in which the mother appears as a mythical figure. The atmosphere here is both solemn, frightening, and mysterious.

JÜNGER: You may be thinking about a dream in which my mother and I are lying in a meadow. The surface of the meadow turns into a green blanket, a kind of counterpane. She grabs the meadow and pulls it over me. It was a dream about death, in a solemn atmosphere, and yet it imbued me with a very powerful confidence. Incidentally, when I was seriously wounded in 1918, for a while I had that pacified feeling of vanishing into half-sleep; and I must admit that I felt I had again grown close to my mother. The first death I ever witnessed was during the war of 1914-1918: a French officer. At that time, in 1915, we were on the outskirts of Verdun, in the *grande tranchée*, and we had to use a road where a French officer was lying on the ground by the side of the road. When I addressed him, he pulled his blanket over his face, nothing interested him anymore.

HERVIER: In *On the Marble Cliffs*, old Lampusa appears as a particularly disquieting incarnation of those mythical figures. One is reminded of Faust and of Goethe's Realm of Mothers.

JÜNGER: The mother evokes Gaia, the ancient goddess, who is not always very reassuring. The domain of Mothers stretches across a vast horizon, from the Furies to the Holy Virgin—and one always finds the serpent yet again. You know that in Goethe's *The Fairy Tale*, a child plays a major role; and the child Erion, whom I introduce in my story in *On the Marble Cliffs*, is not the least bit afraid of snakes, whereas the visitor, Braquemart, who shares certain traits with Goethe, has to get a grip on himself in his rationalism. He certainly passes across the snakes, but he does so with very mixed feelings. When you get away from rationality, the danger increases, instinct weakens. Genius is just the opposite: the child is a genius, every child is a genius. The first attack on his genius occurs when he attends school; I hadn't even begun school, but I already had the impression that it was something highly disagreeable. Evidently, my parents, or the maid, or someone else had threatened me: "Just wait and see when you go to school!" And I thought it was an invention, a mere scarecrow, like the bogeyman. That was what school meant to me, and it didn't really exist. I stood on the balcony of our house in Hanover or in the third-floor apartment that we had rented (my father wasn't earning very much as yet. We lived in a nice neighborhood, but on the third landing: that could seem typical for our social situation). I stared down into the street and watched children passing by with school satchels, and I found that very annoying. I thought to myself: "Perhaps school does exist after all!" And then I mulled it over and said to myself: "My parents deliberately got them to walk by here in order to make me believe it." That was my first philosophical reflection! And I can also add something about the balcony: that was where I also had one of my first historical experiences. For a long time, I thought it had taken place in the nineteenth century; but when I verified it afterwards in history books, I learned that it had taken place in 1901. I was up there on the balcony when a carriage rolled by, a barouche containing a general and several other people. A huge reception in his honor had been organized at the railroad station. He was Count Waldersee, who was called not marshal-in-chief, but Marshal of the World. He had commanded the German troops in China during the Boxer Rebellion. That is my first historical memory.

HERVIER: And what are the primary qualities that you would like to find in your grandchildren, in the children of the future?

JÜNGER: I would say: the ability to get along on their own. I am struck by the fact that each generation inherits the qualities it needs to cope with its time; these qualities are not always very agreeable to the elders, yet they are necessary. These qualities have to be exactly what they are. This reminds me of an anecdote. Some time ago, it was my sad duty to attend the funeral of my friend and former superior Hans Speidel, and I spent the night in Bad Godesberg. On my table, I found a book entitled *Hassidic Tales*, edited, I believe, by Martin Buber. Anyway, I read several anecdotes, one of which I greatly liked, the one about Rabbi Zousya. He said to his audience or to his pupils: "When I go to heaven, I won't be asked whether I lived like Moses, I'll be asked whether I lived like Rabbi Zousya." I consider that essential: everyone has to fulfill what he received at birth; it's the only thing that I can say to those young people. You have to lay out your money advantageously, that is, develop your own capacities to an optimal degree. That's very dangerous, of course, for Rabbi Zousya thought that, as Rabbi Zousya, he had lived according to the law. But what is the law for someone who is born a pickpocket? Nietzsche has an answer for that, naturally, but Rabbi Zousya lived a long time before Nietzsche. After Nietzsche, the matter looks very different, and it becomes very perilous, but that's all I wish to say about this topic.

IV

EROS, DRUGS AND TRANSCENDENCE

Henry Miller.
Drugs and ancient Mexico.
Death in dreams.
The serpent. The Bible.
Christianity today and in the past.

HERVIER: We were talking about the importance of the Realm of Mothers in *On the Marble Cliffs*. On the other hand, it would seem that until Boudour Peri in *Heliopolis*, young women play a minor role in your works. Should we view that as a significant turning point in your evolution?

JÜNGER: Yes, that sounds reasonable, it's symptomatic. In my last novel, which is a kind of detective story, a woman of the early twentieth or late nineteenth century also plays an important role. So it's an increasingly salient tendency.

HERVIER: In *Eumeswil*, little Latifah is utterly charming.

JÜNGER: She certainly is. Often, personal reminiscences take on new life by being expressed in a fictional character. I really was at that hotel, in Agadir, and I had to get a haircut. A very young Arab girl did such a skillful job of it that I asked her her name. She said it was Latifah, and I made use of her name.

HERVIER: You were interested in the eroticism of Henry Miller, whom you specifically cite in *Passage of the Line*.

JÜNGER: You know, if you're dealing with pornography—but I certainly wouldn't care to apply that term *expressis verbis* to Miller—it's something that's always existed. However, it has progressed considerably to the extent that publicity has gotten hold of it. In the old days, it was sold undercover, whereas now it has gained its civil rights in great writing, but I would not say high literature. When I was in Paris, my friend Banine (a woman from the Caucasian Mountains, whose real name was Oum el Banine, and who still meticulously attends to my French correspondence) made me aware of Henry Miller, whose books were still circulating surreptitiously, even in Paris. She had given me one or two of his novels—*Tropic of Cancer*, I believe; and my impression was that Miller had a very precise idea. When faced with the world of machines and its terrible destructiveness, one has to react on the offensive: and a very great force, perhaps the most powerful of all, is Eros. Miller despises the technological world and abandons himself to Eros, but he's the serpent biting into its own tail. To phrase it differently, I would say that he's put his harness on backwards, to the extent that sexuality becomes mechanical in him, losing all its charm. Eroticism has to maintain a numinous element, or else it becomes a sheer automatism, and the technological world can score another victory. In any case, while here, in Germany and elsewhere, the freedom to describe situations and sexual facts is widespread, I feel that I already settled that issue in Paris in 1942. Still, it would really be too bad if we lost the charm that is always exerted by a certain concealment.

HERVIER: Indeed, you wrote in *Passage of the Line* (p. 182): "The second power of the depths is Eros: whenever two beings love one another, they deprive Leviathan of a part of his terrain."

JÜNGER: Eros is one of the greatest fundamental powers. Aphrodite and Dionysus: those are the two forces that are still taken seriously today. Dionysus is still celebrated in the tiniest pub. The irruption of Dionysus must have been something monstrous—the invasion of wine into the Greek world, Asia Minor, with its huge processions. Meanwhile, wine has been domesticated; but at that time, the influence of wine must have been similar to that exerted today, although to a lesser degree, by LSD and drugs of that sort: namely, the establishment of a direct link with divine powers. When you read texts about orgiastic scenes, women who danced with cut-off heads, you are forced to admit that the phenomenon must have been extremely dangerous, until it was controlled, and wine achieved a sacramental value. Incidentally, the relationship to cult is completely appropriate for drugs—peyote, etc.

I don't want to dwell too long on this topic, but since I correspond with chemists who keep abreast of this issue, I also feel that many things in the drug scene have changed. Certain drugs that had—one might say—an expressionist effect have evolved toward gentler and more impressionist actions. But it's risky talking about these things, for you might be dealing with an audience that is not cut out to hear them.

HERVIER: Although in *Approaches*, you devoted an entire book to the problem of wine, intoxication, and drugs, your present attitude seems guarded?

JÜNGER: It's a very slippery terrain. My interest in drugs has caused me various difficulties. But I take drugs too seriously to believe that one should make a habit of them and use them like cigarettes. My example in this area are the Mexicans, who did not take drugs on a daily basis; instead, they got together on certain occasions in order to indulge in them as part of a cult. That was why Christianity had so much trouble converting them. They told the missionaries: "What can we await from your Christ? We encounter our gods repeatedly, we see them, we sit down at the table with them!" I'm profoundly convinced that great intuitions are revealed, but this is not granted to everyone. It may then be desirable to rely on an initiator, a guru, or a priest, who will help you to steady your steps, rather than letting you charge all alone, with a lowered head, into danger. The man who does that by throwing caution to the winds is risking his life.

HERVIER: Isn't that the kind of intuition that you are seeking in dreams?

JÜNGER: I owe a great deal to dreams, and I've recorded many; I'm of the opinion that life in a dream plunges to a greater depth than our daytime vision of the world.

HERVIER: In regard to your parents, you were speaking about your gift for encountering the dead in dreams.

JÜNGER: Yes, but is it really a gift? Isn't it actually a receptiveness? I told you something strange happens with the dead and the houses one dreams about. You find yourself with the dead in houses that were destroyed by bombs a long time ago; you dream like that for ten years, and then it's out of the question. I tell myself that this must involve a posthumous survival of people and places, which then disappear. That was what happened with my grandmother. I've often found myself with her in her house, but today it occurs very seldom, as if there were a second existence, which likewise fades bit by bit, eventually disappearing altogether. There's something ghostly about it.

HERVIER: Haven't you said that there are special moments for those apparitions of the dead?

JÜNGER: It's really quite astonishing. They appear at certain periods, during the twelve nights from Christmas to right after New Year's. That's an experience that many people have, but most of them don't much like to talk about it. It comes up in *Visit to Godenholm*. This was based an a true-life experience: at a certain moment, the moon was rising, and it was like a tremendous irruption.

HERVIER: The protagonist of *Godenholm* is the magus Schwarzenberg—or Nigromontanus.

JÜNGER: Yes, he occasionally pops up in my other books.

HERVIER: Does he have any connection with reality?

JÜNGER: Just like the Great Forester in *On the Marble Cliffs*. Those are dreams that trigger narrative developments. But then, one always looks for the keys.

HERVIER: A little while ago, you mentioned the relationship between the serpent and the Realm of Mothers. This creature has a very special place in your universe.

JÜNGER: The serpent also has a great significance in Nietzsche, who calls it the most intelligent of the animals. Now if you consider this creature purely from an anatomical viewpoint, you are struck by the fact that its brain is fairly undeveloped, compared with those of the primates. But obviously, Nietzsche is thinking of a very different form of intelligence, the closeness to the earth. Nietzsche says that the worst thing is to doubt what the earth wants: and the serpent knows exactly what the earth wants.

Furthermore, the serpent has always fascinated me and troubled me because of its absence of limbs, which constitutes an approach to perfection: for all our limbs and all our senses are actually deviations from a state of perfection. One could also say that our senses deviate from what Angelus Silesius, for instance, calls "sense"—if it is still possible to perceive in the protozoan a great power concentrated on itself. In one-celled organisms, everything is still undifferentiated; as soon as a tiny red dot appears—the eye—something separates from the whole, namely light, and this constitutes the start of a specialization. Once I develop a sense, I am withdrawing something from the totality. This is the same phenomenon that occurs in regard to a limb. That is why the *bios* as a whole always tends toward restoring a state from which limbs are excluded. Thus, all animals that move at a great speed—those that dive, swim, fly—tend to fold their wings along their bodies, they tend toward that absence of limbs. This is also true metaphysically. The Buddha, when he meditates, virtually folds his arms and legs into himself. The posture of prayer consists in crossing your arms and folding your legs underneath you; the hands are not left open, they're joined together—it's a reduction to a less mobile but more perfect state toward which one tends permanently. The serpent in itself constitutes a case of reduction: namely, a reptile that has lost its limbs. And that is why it arouses my fascinated disquiet.

HERVIER: The Bible likewise abounds in prophetic dreams. Is it still as important for you as when you were reading it during the war?

JÜNGER: Indeed, the Bible always has something to offer us. However, mankind sometimes moves away from the Bible at a more or less great distance. That's exactly what happened to me: from that point of view, I had a rather typical relationship to the Bible. As a child, you live in the age of fairy tales, with the three Magi; it all has a highly personal significance. Later on, however—this may have happened when I was almost thirteen—I made the acquaintance of Darwin's system, and I believed that I was now above all that fairy-tale business. I no longer wanted to hear all those padre stories, as you say when you're young. But the process is as follows: once things take an apocalyptic turn, the Bible re-exerts its force on people. However, I wouldn't go so far as to say that I did what Nietzsche describes as "creeping at the foot of the Cross." But all at once, the Bible has more to say to everyone, because you find an array of fundamental situations in it: Jeremiah and Isaiah, the transformation of the world into a desert, the destruction of Babylon and of all those cities makes a vivid impact on the imagination—especially if you think about the annihilation of Dresden. That was why I was particularly interested in the Bible during World War II. During the First World War, I was still a complete atheist. I remember that one day I found myself in front of a trench that was sustaining brisk fire. I had to get across it, and I mused that a prayer would be appropriate. But I told myself: "No, if I didn't care about the Good Lord when everything was going well, it would be awful to ask for his help now!"

To sum it up: during the Second War, I began reading the Bible, and I completed it twice. I personally prefer the parables about miracles, and I still delve into them occasionally. All in all, I proceed according to the following scheme: I read a chapter, then I read the criticism, then I refute it and come up with my own criticism. For instance, take the resurrection of the young man of Nain, that place on the road from Jerusalem to Damascus, which I passed myself, and where the event occurred—or supposedly occurred. First I thought: "That man has now returned to Abraham's bosom, he's in a blissful state. Why bother bringing him back to earth; he'll have little to be thankful for!" Then I told myself that it wasn't a miracle but a parable, and thus a lot more meaningful. Christ tells the mother: "Your son is alive. And he is alive up there, in paradise." But the assistants don't believe him. So Christ has to resurrect the body: it's a pedagogical act. Consequently, you have to view it as such and stick to that. Such was more or less my approach to reading the Bible, and I have to admit that in this way, I got a great deal out of it.

HERVIER: So you feel that the apocalyptic threats facing mankind today demonstrate the full meaning of the Bible?

JÜNGER: Yes, but I have to admit that, if I look at most representatives of our current theology, I see that they have barely gotten into the apocalyptic vision. They're more involved in social issues, which certainly concern them, but only marginally. If ever the whole world blows up, it would be nice to know how we ought to act. When I read the old hymnals, it's very different:

> If the world met its doom,
> I would enter a state of Glory!

That kind of Christian has become very rare! Luther was still like that.

HERVIER: Do you feel that a new form of religiosity could emerge?

JÜNGER: A lot of things would have to happen in the upper spheres. In any case, it won't be due to a simple effort of our will.

V

SUBTLE HUNTS AND PLANETARY VOYAGES

Entomology.
Scientific data.
Destruction of the environment.
In the tropics. Praise of the Third World.
Heidegger. The naturalist's renown. Picasso.

HERVIER: You once planned to devote yourself to the natural sciences. And you therefore studied zoology at Leipzig and Naples. What do the natural sciences signify in your life today?

JÜNGER: The decision I made after World War I to go and study at Leipzig for two years was based on things that turned out to be not very solid. I had launched into those studies under the influence of the old botanists and zoologists, and I expected a bumper crop of images. But instead, I was inundated by numbers and figures. You can see it very clearly in the scientific journals. For instance, take ornithology, the study of birds: the old scientists, like Alfred Brehm's father or Neumann, stood out because of the richness of their vision. Today, all that is replaced with a terrifying quantity of figures, a plenitude of figures, which tends increasingly toward measurement down to the last millimeter. People use devices to catch the singing of birds, with that modern-day mania for always resorting to machines to help us out; and they measure phenomena and masses down to the micron. Their activity gets more and more detailed, and it's overwhelmed with a gloomier and gloomier boredom. This is a revolution that's inherent in the era itself, a revolution that is experienced by everybody. What you are offered does not correspond in any way to what you expect. That was why I bade farewell to zoology. I now study it privately, out in the woods and fields. I'm passionately fond of organisms, and this kind of research brings me infinitely more.

HERVIER: You seem to prefer a science of nature in Goethe's sense of the term, in which phenomenology takes precedence over data.

JÜNGER: Obviously, toward the mid-nineteenth century, a revolution occurred. After Goethe, one could still find geographers, geologists, and botanists—like Fechner, for example—who continued to be interested in organisms in their totality, without forgetting the reverse. But all that is gradually fading in a pure world of figures.

HERVIER: And now you note the disappearance of numerous animal species. Isn't that an enormous threat to the future of the planet?

JÜNGER: Of course; it's highly regrettable, and it's become almost impossible to open a newspaper without finding lamentations about that topic. When I arrived in Wilflingen, I specialized in the study of coleopterans; there were a huge number of species which no longer exist now. I often say that my collection has taken on a sort of pale-ontological value. In *Subtle Hunts*, I talked about living in Egypt, in Nubia, at a hotel surrounded by a beautiful garden cascading with flowers, and I thought I would find ample booty. But when I examined my butterfly net, I found almost nothing, and I very quickly realized why. I saw an enormous Nubian dressed all in red and armed with an enormous sprayer to kill weeds and vermin—or at least what is called vermin, if you believe people, for an entomologist has very different value judgments. Anyway, this man was spraying DDT or some other poison everywhere, and there was nothing left. Along came an American woman, who saw me with my insect bottle, and she asked me what I was doing. I told her that I was hunting coleopterans. "Oh," she cried, "then I can't shake your hand." She went on her way and ran into that good gardener with his sprayer; and she shook his hand. I consider that a very typical example. A man kills millions of living creatures, and people shake his hand; another man wants to achieve a precise vision of several species, and people refuse to shake his hand. It's somewhat like shaking hands with the man who works on the atomic bomb, but being suspicious of the man who works with a rifle, as I had to do for a certain time.

HERVIER: Your ecological orientation must inspire a certain sympathy for the Greens?

JÜNGER: I can't deny it. I tend to think that they're on the right path: perhaps like Faust's famulus, who wanted to know everything, but had not yet put his knowledge in order. This could certainly happen if first-rate personalities emerged from those circles. In any case, there is something that you have been able to note and that I dwell on in my book *The Worker*: namely, that pure economy is not enough. We are therefore sent from economy to ecology. That's a first step, but of course it's not the last. Nevertheless, I insist that it's a step in the right direction.

HERVIER: Your vast travels allow you to pursue your great passion for the "subtle hunt" in all corners of the world.

JÜNGER: I'm interested in a great many things, including zoology and botany. If you're interested in very small animals, the world promptly becomes immense. That is still a way of savoring it in terms of a very different extension: a small dune or a bush becomes a microcosm, which you can focus on for a very long time. I often travel in the tropics or in subtropical regions, and I spend whole hours with a single blossoming bush: the world grows.

HERVIER: What are your favorite destinations?

JÜNGER: I need to visit Paris two or three times a year and the Mediterranean coast at least once. On the one hand, that gives me the social and intellectual energy I require. And on the other hand, it gives me the plunge into nature that is just as necessary for me. However, tropical trips also have their importance for me; I felt very good on the shores of the Amazon, but I've been learning, alas, that there too, the devastation is proceeding apace. This year, I may go to Sumatra, where one of my fellow entomologists, Dr. Diehl, is head of a hospital. He has invited me very warmly, and I find the idea of that trip quite seductive.

HERVIER: In dealing with extremely diverse civilizations, are you, above all, sensitive to the infinite variety of human behavior, or are you struck primarily by the underlying unity of man?

JÜNGER: Each country contains part of the primordial substance that we call "fatherland," and I like to come up with that kind of integrity. This can happen anywhere, even in the desert.

HERVIER: Isn't that substance best preserved in the countries of the

Third World, where life has retained a naturalness and simplicity that we no longer know?

JÜNGER: Naturally, but those people are being invaded more and more by our civilization, which is alien to them. In any case, the mere fact that the British and the Americans, and those who call themselves the "Whites"—the mere fact that they use the term "underdeveloped" is scandalous. They want to develop the "underdeveloped" countries by inculcating them with our own mistakes. Everyone has to own two cars in order to be considered developed. If every Chinese person owned a car, pollution would reach astronomical proportions. To my mind, a nation is infinitely more developed if it respects its own inherent tribal customs. They want to take them away from a Nomos that is in keeping with them, and they want to impose another one, for which we ourselves are beginning to suffer. So when I travel, I want to get to know countries that are the same as they have always been. That was still the case in Angola, for instance: in Liberia, I was enthroned as an "honorable chief!" The Blacks had heard that their guest was a man who had distinguished himself in the two wars, and they were impressed, while such a reaction is unthinkable in our world. And they had a great celebration in my honor. However, I am experiencing once again what I told you in regard to the Foreign Legion: I spend my time chasing after that authenticity. I make the acquaintance of a very beautiful country, I wish to return there, and meanwhile it has been considerably devastated by tourism. In 1932, I really loved Rhodesia; but if you go back now, all you find is high-rises. Lake Victoria, which was discovered by Stanley, is now thoroughly polluted by all the industries along its banks. Thus, today, traveling has become a constant escape—a flight from the reality of the moment. You have to go to places where the world is not yet destroyed: it's a hunt for the ideal, a phantom. Yet travel is one the few domains where technology is positive. It is a ray of sunshine in the present-day world: you can swiftly reach countries which people could only dream about in the past.

HERVIER: *À propos* of traveling, you talk about Heidegger, who was more of a homebody. You know that he was once invited to give a lecture in Rome, where he was supposed to spend a week. But the lecture was such a big hit that he was asked to give a second one, and he spent his entire stay indoors, preparing the lecture.

JÜNGER: Yes: in *Seventy Wanes*, I quote a letter that Heidegger wrote me, saying that he is like an old Chinese, he prefers staying at home. My brother Friedrich Georg was closer to Heidegger than I, and he always had anecdotes about him. One day, Heidegger was stung in the back of the neck by a bee, and my brother told him that that was excellent for rheumatism. Heidegger didn't know what to answer. I have a whole pack of letters that he sent me, and he also presented me with two unpublished essays in a very beautiful penmanship. He gave seminars on *The Worker* and *Total Mobilization*. If only he hadn't done those stupid things—for which, however, I don't reproach him; it is not the job of the philosopher to have clear political thinking. Besides, the situation was not such that one could say: "I want to preserve things as they are." He thought that something new was coming, but he was dreadfully mistaken. He did not have as clear a vision as I did.

HERVIER: Don't you feel that your activity as a naturalist will contribute, along with your work as a writer, to your survival for posterity?

JÜNGER: Since you care to bestow on me that honorific title of naturalist, I will reply that when one has the opportunity of giving one's name to an insect, a bird, a beetle, one enjoys a posthumous glory that generally endures longer than that of a writer. It will last as long as the Linnaean system. In this domain, I see a whole series of happy prospects opening before me. Not only have a half dozen or more beetles been named after me, but also butterflies and shell fish. My friend Théodoridès even dedicated a one-celled organism to me, *Gregarina jungeri*. Furthermore, there is a subspecies of tiger beetles called *jungerella*. It's a family of beetles that I particularly appreciate; they are animals that run along the sand, you've probably observed them on the beach. I was fascinated by them even as a child; perhaps they correspond to the way I move: these animals remain motionless, then they spot a goal and they race toward it, and then they freeze back into their immobility. You can see that all this was very auspicious. And for posthumous literary glory, I don't set excessive store by it. I'm skeptical, for I've observed that such glory pales even in an author's lifetime. He then leads the life of a *pauvre poète oublié* [a poor forgotten poet]. Or else he behaves very sensibly, like Rimbaud, who, after producing an exceptional literary oeuvre in his youth, devoted himself to commerce in Africa; that was more important in his eyes. And *sub specie aeternitatis*, the day will come when even Homer will be totally unknown. Glory is like the blazing tail of a comet, which still sparkles for a while in the wake of the work. You may then wonder what the goal of writing is, assuming it has a goal. It is the creative instant itself, in which something timeless is produced, something that cannot be wiped out. The universe has affirmed itself in the individual, and that must suffice, whether or not anyone else notices it. In 1942, when I visited Picasso on Rue des Grands-Augustins, he said to me: "Look, this painting, which I have just completed, is going to have a certain effect; but this effect would be exactly the same, metaphysically speaking, if I wrapped the painting up in paper and consigned it to a corner. It would be exactly the same thing as if ten thousand people had admired it." And he added something that I particularly liked: "If the two of us had the power to negotiate peace, Paris could be illuminated tonight." And that's always how it is: two people who meet on a street corner or in a bus know how to deal with the issue of disarmament and the atomic bomb. But on a higher level, there seem to be blockages that are almost impossible to overcome.

VI

THE FAMILIAR WORLD

Dialogues. The Stauffenberg House.
Swabian villages. Prussian Spirit.
A day. Magic objects.
Hourglasses. Astrology. Paintings.

HERVIER: Here we are, engaged in a long dialogue, and I haven't even had a chance to thank you for agreeing to it.

JÜNGER: My dear man, the situation is as follows: every man has numerous friends and acquaintances, with whom he gets on. Some of them have enough of a literary and historical background for him to talk with them. And yet, despite everything, a dialogue cannot always ensue. These things are hard to explain; it's a question of music, of a certain harmony. Two intelligent people can meet, they can like each other; but nevertheless, a euphonious contact fails to emerge. The laws of a certain magnetism have to come into play. There are even extreme cases in which too much liking induces a blockage. Stendhal explained it very well in *On Love*: even when the crystallization does not take place, two people can still readily like each other very much. Now you and I recently met in Paris, where we had one of those outstanding conversations, which are generally few and far between. I'm no great fan of all those birthday affairs. But after all, since the celebration of my ninetieth birthday had to take place, it would be better not to run the risk of failure. That was why I invited you; and I am delighted to welcome you in Wilflingen, in the house of the Great Forester.

HERVIER: This place has an exceptional aura in more ways than one. Not only does it touch on literature by evoking the character who stands up to the forces of evil in *On the Marble Cliffs*, but it is also tied to its owners, the great family of the Stauffenbergs.

JÜNGER: Naturally, it struck me as a bizarre coincidence when I was offered the chance to live in the home of the Great Forester, where I have now been residing for thirty-four years. Across the road, you can see the castle of the Stauffenbergs. It does not belong to the same branch of the family as the leader of the plot against Hitler. The two branches separated about one hundred twenty years ago, I believe. But simply because of their name, they were included in a collective family responsibility and faced a great danger. If you look at the door, you can still make out the traces of the seals that the Gestapo placed there. The family members were kept prisoner in that house, and the trial documents were stored here. The Gestapo thugs regularly discussed the questions they would have to ask the next day. However, there is a kind of Ear of Denys in that room. You know that in Syracuse, the tyrant Denys employed a special, ear-shaped rock, through which he could eavesdrop on what his prisoners were telling one another. Here, the Denys Ear functions vertically: anything said in that room can be heard up there, under the roof. So the Stauffenberg children could regularly inform their parents about the questions they would be asked the next day.

Furthermore, in early 1945, that house served as a residence for the members of the French government who were interned here, or lodged, if you prefer. You probably know Céline's novel *Castle to Castle*. Marshal Pétain was put up at Sigmaringen and Monsieur Laval lived here. He asked the farmers questions about agriculture, and they still remember him today. I don't need to tell you, but *entre nous*, Laval performed great services for the French. Without him, Hitler would have come down on your country with extreme cruelty. In certain cases, somebody has to remain, to keep everything from going up in fire and smoke.

The first visitors I received here were Madame Laval and Countess de Chambrum. They went on a sort of pilgrimage to all the places where the unfortunate Laval stayed before his execution. Hence, this place is not without a certain historic aura; perhaps we've increased this aura in the course of thirty-four years; it imbues all the walls.

HERVIER: You chose to live in a village.

JÜNGER: In our time, a village is more conducive to the productivity of a man pursuing an intellectual activity than a big city; although you have to consider the fact that the difference between town and country seems to be blurring. For instance, it would take me two hours to get from here to Paris if I didn't have the long trip to the Stuttgart airport, then from Orly to Paris. The famous media send us the news with a swiftness that no one would have dared to dream of in the past. So we can't say that we live here the way Erasmus and so many others did, in a cell, a hermitage. But life in the Swabian villages remains very pleasant.

HERVIER: Your affinities with the Prussian spirit did not seem to predispose you for living in Swabia.

JÜNGER: True, but you know the Swabians are called the Prussians of southern Germany. I particularly appreciate their excellent attitude towards the German language. The Swabians are considered the most brilliant branch of the German family. We live very close to Tübingen, where the thinking minds of the *Stift* went to school: there were whole classes of geniuses. And you can still notice it in the villages, where the people speak an excellent German. I would even say, if I may be permitted, that the people in Wilflingen speak a better German than the teachers in Tübingen; and I learn a great deal from conversations with neighbors. I often hear certain sentence constructions; I go up to my library and I find those constructions in Fischer, which is the dictionary of the Swabian language. So I have an opportunity to keep learning.

HERVIER: How would you define the Prussian spirit?

JÜNGER: The image that people have of the Prussians can generally be viewed as an intelligence test. Usually, the Prussians are as disgraced as the Spartans. A lot of people hate the Spartans while others admire them. In the Prussians, the Eastern and Western influences are probably so well balanced that a system of command and obedience, and joyous helpfulness function harmoniously. If history is not more bland and uniform than it appears today, we owe it in part to the Prussians and the Japanese, who have remained faithful to the *Nomos*. But one barely has the right to say so today.

HERVIER: Could you retrace the course of one of your normal days?

JÜNGER: There is nothing special about my daily schedule. I get up around nine o'clock, I take a bath, and its temperature is that of the water coming from the faucet. At the moment, it's five degrees Centigrade [forty degrees Fahrenheit]. So I can't stay in very long, but I emerge thoroughly revived. Then I have breakfast and open my mail; it keeps swelling and becoming more and more copious. Incidentally, I get as many letters from France as I do from Germany. I never eat lunch, for I've noticed that a noontime meal leaves me drowsy. In any case, after eating, I'm incapable of carrying out any original creative activity. However, an author's life does not consist purely in immediate production. Otherwise, one hour would be more than enough; but there are visitors, relations with neighbors, for instance with the bibliophiles of Upper Swabia. There are still old texts to be found in the surrounding castles, for instance those of Count Bodman and so many others; this is extremely stimulating. Then comes reading. I read a lot: for me, a day without reading is a lost day. In the evening, I read till midnight; and if there's anything fascinating about the material, then I may even read till dawn. Now that's a normal day for me.

HERVIER: What is your relationship to the present times? Do you read the newspaper, do you watch television?

JÜNGER: My precise relationship to the present is very hard to pinpoint. Naturally, I'm obliged to keep abreast of events. So I regularly listen to the television news. I read the newspapers, but in a spotty fashion, as it were, and sometimes I go through the illustrated magazines, because I'm interested in finding out what other people are interested in. So let's say that I keep more or less up to date. As for pure politics, my book *Author and Authorship* explained quite clearly that to my mind, political participation can only damage what is essential in a writer. However, there is an entirely different "currentness"—namely, the cosmic situation we find ourselves in; and in politics, there are certain phenomena that derive from the idea that pure economy is no longer sufficient. There are environmental problems that transcend politics and involve wider contexts. That was the focus of my book *The Wall of Time*, which received scant attention, but I have to avoid feeling any irritation. If we believe, or accept the hypothesis, that a cyclical order exists, this hypothesis goes beyond the notion of progress. Progress is linear, while cyclical movements return to their starting points. One could therefore say that a kind of panic recurs once every thousand years. Around the year 1000, people feared the end of the world. This is again the case today, when the omens are technological, while in earlier times they were religious: people are afraid of the atomic bomb. For my part, I don't believe in any great danger.

HERVIER: In your *Parisian Journal*, you describe Braque's studio. It's strewn with objects that look like talismans, and that seem to have a magical value for him. You yourself live surrounded by engravings, seashells, beautiful or curious objects.

JÜNGER: The snake you see over the bookshelves comes from a set of drawings that were done for Louis XIV: it's in the collections of the Louvre. I ordered it at the engraving studio, and then I had it colored. It reproduces exactly the posture of the stuffed snake above it. At its side, there's a small god sculpted from an elephant tusk—a present that I was given in Liberia, when I was made a tribal chieftain. And to the left, I have my collection of hourglasses.

I was instantly fascinated with hourglasses, because I was preoccupied with the issue of time. The hourglass measures time in a different way, the way of elementary timepieces, like sun dials and water clocks. They're completely different from clocks with gears and escarpments. And I consider it very remarkable that we are returning to elementary clocks with our quartz watches—that is, sand watches. We measure with the atom, which is also something highly materialistic. Materialism contains a prodigious depth that materialists are still a long way from fully grasping. As people go into the twenty-first century, this situation will have every opportunity to change considerably as we enter the Age of Aquarius.

HERVIER: You seem almost as interested in astrology as you are in science. In fact, you discuss it at great length in *The Wall of Time*, which you cited a short while ago.

JÜNGER: Yes, astrology is rooted in a very ancient lore, next to which I might possibly put the art of chess and other phenomena of that ilk. It's a different way of combining things, but since everything in the world forms a coherent whole, this too has to make sense. Naturally, I could devise some kind of soothsaying—in coffee grounds or whatever; it's impossible for that not to have some form of accuracy. But one should simply not reduce everything to a purely personal destiny. When I note something that allows me to state: "The world is in order," my personal misfortune can quite easily be an integral part of that order. That is the attitude of the tragic poet.

HERVIER: One sometimes has the impression that good or bad luck belongs to each individual as a sort of intrinsic quality.

JÜNGER: Certainly. The important thing is to remain faithful to one's style. You can say that Mussolini's end was dreadful; but remember the end of Vitellius. If I wish to lead the life of a caesar, I must accept dying like Vitellius, who was dragged through the Tiber on a hook. Memories are very strong in Mussolini's case, especially the fact that the executioners were the same people who had cheered him the previous day. Too much luck is always suspect.

HERVIER: In many of the works surrounding you, one feels the presence of an almost magical element, the closeness of a destiny. For instance, who is the child depicted here?

JÜNGER: You see here an illustration representing Erion, by the painter Nay au Mans. Nay was a "degenerate artist," whom I had a chance to help out in France; I was able to obtain a certain amount of protection for him by the commander-in-chief. This is *The Voyeur*: the voyeur is spying on a loving couple. This painting strikes me as typical of Expressionism: the lovers are virtually exploding towards an enormous full moon that has risen over the countryside. Kubin also gave me a painting and several beautiful drawings. This is the *Meeting in the Forest*: a *Waldgänger* [forest stroller] comes upon an eagle. Kubin wrote a very lovely dedication on it.

HERVIER: And this painting, which we see in front of your desk?

JÜNGER: This is a picture of the home of the fallen cuirassier in *A Dangerous Encounter* on Rue du Cherche-Midi, at the corner of Rue du Regard. The house was destroyed, and it's been replaced by an idiotic construction. A painter named Mohr offered to do a painting of a corner of Paris that I particularly liked; and I asked him to paint this house, on the corner of Rue du Regard. Next to it is *Atlantis Before the Catastrophe* by Schlichter. As for the steel helmet, that's the one I wore in my very first tank battle; I turned back to my men at the exact moment that the bullet veered through my helmet; you can still see the blood stains. The helmet had an excellent shape; today's helmets aren't as good.

VII

NAZISM

The Worker and the totalitarian worlds.
Ernst Niekisch. Nazism. Hitler.
Goebbels. *On the Marble Cliffs*.
The assassination attempt of 20 July 1944.
Terrorism. Final war experience.

HERVIER: Can you still recall the period when you wrote *The Worker*, and your view of the world during that phase of your life?

JÜNGER: It must have been around the year 1930 when I began dealing with these issues. I see *The Worker* as a mythical figure making his entrance into our world; the issues of the nineteenth century, which essentially involve economy, have only a secondary interest for me. That is to say: the person who holds the power in his quality of a Titan, naturally also possesses the money. I was also interested in those questions of power in a short narrative, *Aladdin's Problem*.

The important thing in *The Worker* is vision. The gist is a grandeur that is neither economic nor political, but quasi-mythological: the age of the gods is over, and we are entering the age of the titans. This is obvious everywhere. People behave exactly as I analyzed the situation, but they're annoyed if you point it out to them. They want to be seen as lovers of mankind or as Marxists, but in reality, they are mere holders of power: which, incidentally, I prefer—a question of upbringing, no doubt! What irks me is that they claim they're playing a certain role, whereas they've been cast in an entirely different role. Furthermore, in one sense, they play it very well.

HERVIER: Did you consciously see a link between *The Worker* and the situation of the Soviet Union in 1934?

JÜNGER: In 1934, certainly; but it went back to 1917. For example, I was very interested in the plan, the idea of the plan. I told myself: granted, they have no constitution, but they do have a plan. This may be an excellent thing. The influence exerted on me was purely pragmatic. I have always had a certain sense of political phenomena, of states, societies, religious communities, to the extent that I am touched by the factor of order. For instance, I read all twenty-two volumes of Saint-Simon very thoroughly. I am not particularly drawn to a figure like Louis XIV, but I am to his court, the disposition of that court—it's like watching a puppet show. I could say the same thing about the Prussian army, the Jesuit order, the British navy, and certain caesars. At times, history seems to crystallize in highly instructive examples. So it's a good thing that this or that took place. In many ways, history was not as people wished it to be; but there was this crystal, these right angles, this gold standard, which have always fascinated me. For instance, as a Protestant, as a Prussian, as a German, I do not always feel in agreement with history. Yet one can accept one's complete opposite—for example, a figure like Léon Bloy, who is quite frankly my opposite. And I have always been impressed by the things that happen up there, at the top of the tower.

HERVIER: During the period when you were writing *The Worker*, you were very close to Ernst Niekisch, a major representative of "national Bolshevism," who paid dearly for his resistance to Hitler.

JÜNGER: I did know him very well, but it was actually my brother who was friends with him. Niekisch was somewhat in the same situation as the Greens today. He was completely on the right path, and if I may put it this way, he would have been capable of pushing the evolution towards the left: and that would have gained him a far stronger consensus, particularly in the East. Compared with him, Hitler did cheap work, and that was what brought him that monstrous popularity. During that period, I realized that Niekisch was in great danger. He had already published his book, *Hitler: A Misfortune for Germany*, with illustrations by Paul Weber: in it, you see enormous crowds bogged down in a swamp. In this sense, he was very ill-fated, greatly threatened, and I told him: "Why don't you seek refuge in Switzerland. It makes no sense staying here and playing the martyr. It won't help you at all, and no one will be grateful to you; you're in an awful predicament. On the other hand, if you bide your time, things will work out for you." When I was in Paris during the war, the counterespionage services had a whole bunch of people who came from Niekisch's camp. And we would say: "Yes, if Niekisch gets out of prison, he may be able to make statements towards working out a peace." But when Niekisch was finally released, he had become thoroughly incapable of any sustained efforts. He was once again in a terrible predicament. I attended his funeral. There was no major personality there, from either the West or the East. You saw old militants who seemed to come straight out of a Joseph Conrad novel, *The Secret Agent*, basket cases, and a few old friends like Drexel. It was a dismal funeral.

HERVIER: You helped his family out during the Nazi period.

JÜNGER: Yes, to the extent that it was possible. For instance, my brother Hans took in Niekisch's wife and son for a while—that sort of help. But there was very little one could do. I remember that on the day before the trial, I ran all over Berlin. I believe he had a female attorney defending him. I called her. She described that hopeless situation in all its sadness. I managed to contact people in uniform and civilians, and who were all very well disposed towards Niekisch. But none of them wanted to burn their fingers. That's how it was!

HERVIER: What was your position on the Nazi movement during its early stages?

JÜNGER: At first, obviously, they had a whole series of right ideas. That was what brought them their initial success. For example, the fact that they wanted to broadly challenge the Treaty of Versailles and its consequences. Naturally, this struck me as an excellent idea. But the way it was implemented made me more and more uneasy, and in fact, I did not distance myself from it until after Crystal Night. These were things that deeply repelled me and that were, among other things, at the source of my conception of *On the Marble Cliffs*. I depicted the situation there—in a mythical fashion, of course, but very precisely, and the people who were aimed at certainly felt aimed at.

HERVIER: When did you clearly perceive the demonic element in Hitler?

JÜNGER: I still don't know if there was true demonism in his case: that might have been even more brutal. But there were already physiognomic attractions and repulsions. From the very outset, Hitler's physiognomy struck me as equivocal.

HERVIER: Have you ever in your life met a politician who truly impressed you with his qualities?

JÜNGER: Hmm, you know that I'm passionately interested in history, and it is possible—even if I lived in ancient times—that I have never met one who truly impressed me. History often embellishes its material, and the horrible episodes disappear. I don't know how our era will be judged in the year 3000. Perhaps they will say that it was the period of the Hundred Years' War, a war that began in 1914. We're always at war; it's called a cold war, but there is no real peace. Apparently, it is impossible to conclude a peace in the present situation. We have to achieve one world, but it seems terribly difficult.

HERVIER: You knew Goebbels very well: he tried to enroll you in his propaganda enterprise.

JÜNGER: Yes. Later on, Goebbels told someone: "We offered Ernst Jünger golden bridges, but he didn't want to cross them." Actually, my instinctive reaction was excellent. Goebbels too was a man of instinct, but, if I may say so, on a lower level. In 1945, right before the total collapse of National Socialism, when I was about to celebrate my fiftieth birthday, on March 29, Goebbels, in one of his last short speeches, ordered the press not to mark my birthday and especially not to mention it in any newspaper. Apparently, he thought he'd be damaging me. If he had drummed up a lot of hoopla, as they say, he would have hurt me a lot more. But people are incapable of considering their own deaths in their reckonings.

Incidentally, things like that keep recurring. I was thinking of the occasion of the Goethe Prize. I could expect various reactions, and I told myself that the situation would be repeated at intervals of twenty or thirty years. At that time, I was no conformist, I have never been one, nor did I become one in 1982. This can only be to my advantage *sub specie aeternitatis*.

HERVIER: May I quote you? On June 14, 1934, you wrote in the Nazi Party newspaper, *Der Völkische Beobachter*: "My efforts are aimed at preventing even the slightest suspicion of ambiguity about the nature of my political substance."

JÜNGER: Perfectly: but I wouldn't do it again today. I made myself fairly vulnerable. And *à quoi ça peut servir* [what good would it do]? I would willingly ask the question. Today, my mindset is that of an anarch, who says: "Go ahead, but as for me, I'm keeping quiet." But anyway, I did it. Actually, I had largely forgotten about it; there are a whole series of proclamations along those lines. Incidentally, it was a Jewish researcher named Wulf who dug up all that business in the Prussian archives—especially the stories concerning the *Pour le mérite* decoration—and he published them in a book entitled *Literature in the Third Reich*. I appear there as a *rara avis*, in a class by myself; he cites a number of analogous items. Those are things that one forgets. But today, as I've said, I see all that from very far away, and I would act more prudently.

HERVIER: When *On the Marble Cliffs* was published, you could have been in serious jeopardy.

JÜNGER: Naturally, I can't really talk about good luck, but there have always been moments of turbulence that might cause particularly difficult situations. In regard to my novel, I corrected the proofs after putting on my old uniform. The public reception was instantly very ardent. But when the publisher sent me my mail (I was mobilized as a captain in Westphalia), I had a very new impression that a large printing could be disagreeable. My publisher, Hanseatische Verlagsanstalt, wrote me that fourteen thousand copies had been sold in two weeks. I was far from enchanted by this news or by the explicit interpretations made in Switzerland and other neutral countries. Less than four weeks after the publication of *On the Marble Cliffs*, there was a conference of *Reichsleiters*; and the *Reichsleiter* of Lower Saxony—if I'm not mistaken, his name was Bouhler—said to Hitler: "My Führer, we can't go on like this with that Ernst Jünger, this whole business of *On the Marble Cliffs*!" The word spread, and right away, the novel was specifically applied to Nazism, far more specifically than I had foreseen. My brother Friedrich Georg had been the first to read the book, and he had said: "In my opinion, they're going to either ban it within six weeks, or let it go." And his prediction was right on target. The *Reichsleiter* complained to Hitler, who replied that I was to be left alone. That was luck! Thus I had a very privileged position, which allowed me to do a lot of things that would have turned out very badly if other people had done them. And during the war, if you were in the army, you tended to be protected, at least until the assassination attempt of the Twentieth of July. We smelled trouble, but then we very quickly evacuated Paris.

HERVIER: What consequences did the events of July 1944 have for you?

JÜNGER: I experienced them in the eye of the cyclone, as it were. But I must say that in all difficult situations, I have always found people who came to my aid. They may be people one hardly knows. Later on, I got hold of the files of the top SS leaders. They contained the names of completely unknown people who protected me. For example, at the Raphael, the head SS man, who was supposed to perform other functions, used to have lunch with us. After the Twentieth of July 1944, the thugs of Avenue Foch, the Gestapo headquarters, pointed out that there were two extremely dangerous men in Stülpnagel's entourage; "The first is Pastor Damrath, and the second that Captain Jünger; both men's dossiers must be examined very carefully." The head of the SS then said: "I eat lunch with Jünger every day, he's lost in his dreams. He's sort of a poet or goodness knows what. There's nothing to be gotten out of him!" His reaction was very useful to me. The evening of July 20, when we all got together behind doubly closed doors, Captain Hattingen, one of my comrades, said to me: "We had the giant serpent in our bag, and we let it go!" Some of the men wanted to shoot all the SS men; but Stülpnagel was incapable of that. If it had been someone in the other camp, he wouldn't have felt the same scruples.

HERVIER: In *Heliopolis*, you clearly explained your hostility to assassinations. What is your reaction to current terrorism?

JÜNGER: That's obviously a burning question. But to deal with assassinations from a more general perspective, I was prompted in the course of studying history to view assassinations as attempts to change the course of history by means that are inappropriate to it, elementary means. That is why the results of most assassinations are the direct opposite of what the conspirators intended: thus, they harm themselves, independently of the personal risk they run. That was true of the Fieschi plot, which you are, no doubt, acquainted with. Fieschi built an infernal machine to kill Louis-Philippe and his escort. He set up thirty guns parallel with one another, and a few exploded, ripping off his hand. But that was merely a secondary mishap. In any case, the event helped to shore up Louis-Philippe's administration for another fifteen years. The same could be said about the attempt on Lenin's life: it led to a huge massacre in the educated circles and did more good than harm to Bolshevism. In fact, I have the impression that when the ruling power begins to get shaky, it welcomes such assassination attempts. Nevertheless, we have to make distinctions. Harmodius and Aristogiton, for instance, are of a different format.

HERVIER: In Roman history, one could illustrate that distinction with the example of the two Brutuses. But we were talking about present-day terrorism.

JÜNGER: It arouses neither my sympathy nor my antipathy: it's really a question of historical observation. In my novel *Eumeswil*, the reader meets a human type who prefers to observe. I would therefore say that terrorists differ from anarchists in that the latter have a precise goal: for instance, they want to strike down a prince or blow up a palace, while the terrorist aims at creating a general climate of fear.

In evaluating the symptoms, one could say that the increase of terrorism reveals an overall disorganization of things. So I see terrorism more as a symptom, a general attitude that attests to a lack of harmony.

HERVIER: For terrorism to make sense, it would have to have public opinion on its side.

JÜNGER: Certainly. One could say that Sand's assassination of Kotzebue virtually legitimized Metternich's policies. It led to censorship measures and all kinds of unpleasant consequences, which lasted practically until 1848.

HERVIER: It's also a moral issue: Is it legitimate for an individual to impose his will on the majority by means of violence?

JÜNGER: Clearly not. But it can produce an overall electrical tension. Certain wires burn spontaneously. For instance, that sort of atmosphere prevailed when Damiens tried to assassinate Louis XV. Damiens bore a slight resemblance to the hero of *Eumeswil*, but he was plainly more stupid. He thought that if Louis XV were killed, then everything would improve. Incidentally, one must also consider the issue of hypertension in Damiens. The evening before the attempt, he wandered about, looking for a surgeon to bleed him. Afterwards, he said: "If I had found a surgeon, the assassination attempt would not have taken place." The question of age also plays a role. One seldom encounters aged assassins. This also applies to terrorists on the whole: you will find very few who become old, after escaping all the dangers, which inevitably include suicide.

HERVIER: Getting back to the assassination attempt of the Twentieth of July, you were not directly harassed.

JÜNGER: And fortunately the fact that there were public readings of *Peace* at Rommel's headquarters, and that it was discussed there did not come out. Next, the Wehrmacht was very glad to get rid of me. When I returned to Hanover, I had to report to the regional command. I went to find the colonel, a man named Urhahn, who asked me what I wished to do. I replied that the situation looked bad, and that little could be done: I didn't care to seek the limelight. And he answered: "Fine, okay, I'll transfer you to the reserve. Call me every two weeks." I told myself that this was not a bad solution. But one week later, he summoned me to headquarters and announced to me that Keitel had called to find out what was becoming of me. And he warned him that he ought to get rid of me. That was what gave rise to the myth that I was thrown out of the Wehrmacht. It's incorrect. I requested my discharge in a perfectly regular manner: I reported sick. The physician stated that I had gastric and other complications, which is done in such cases; and so I received my discharge in due form.

However, I was instantly made head of the territorial militia, as Volkssturmführer, in the Burgdorf region. I went there and reported to the Kreisleiter, the head of the region: I asked him how things were going, and what I was to do, and he said to me: "Put up an anti-tank barrage, destroy a couple of tanks for us, and send them packing!"

I heard him out. And he added: "Do you know that because of you I nearly wound up in the guardhouse?"

"That's impossible, sir," I said. "But it's true," he said, "you were in the Harz Mountains, in Blankenburg, when you were mobilized. You were walking across the grounds of the barracks, where I had been sent as a recruit; and my warrant officer said, 'That's Captain Jünger crossing the grounds: do you know him?' 'No, sir,' I replied, 'I don't.' 'Then you ought to be thrown in jail instantly!'" The *Kreisleiter* told me the story because he had been so deeply impressed; and I'm repeating it to you only to show you the atmosphere, the situation I found myself in. Thus, I could take certain liberties. Naturally, I destroyed no tanks. In the neighboring village, members of the Hitler Youth wiped out an American tank. The immediate result was that the entire village was burned down. I told my boys: "The instant we spot the first American soldiers, I'll open the barrage, and then just get out of here! . . ." And that was what they did. As for me, I was visited by an American colonel who had read some of my books, and so the transition was very gentle. The Americans were followed by the British, who were billeted in the presbytery of Kirchhorst. A [British] officer named Stuart Hood was one of my "occupiers." He read *On the Marble Cliffs* and translated it, so that I owe a remarkable translation to that invader.

VIII

THE ANARCH, POLITICS AND COMMITMENT

Non-conformity. The anarch.
Stirner, Kirkegaard. The rebel. *Eumeswil*.
The diehard observer. Commitment.

HERVIER: Aside from Nazism, you've experienced various political regimes. Yet you seem to have been ill at ease under all of them.

JÜNGER: I lived under the Empire, the First Republic, the Third Reich, and now I'm in the Second Republic. But I must say that in regard to forms of government, on a certain level of my life, my function is that of the anarch. I have never felt any identity with any regime. That's rather significant. At eighteen, I fled to the Foreign Legion; and when I was there, I deserted. Luckily, I always sensed that this was no coincidence. I've already told you about my unpleasant dealings with dear Goebbels, and the way the situation was repeated when I put up with all those attacks upon being awarded the Goethe Prize. It's not very pleasant, but in a powerful sense, it constitutes a sort of alibi. Thirty years from now, people will say that at the time, Jünger was not a conformist going along with people who will be judged very differently. At first, the Germans were intent on assuming and overcoming the responsibilities for the Second World War; but perhaps someday they will overcome the things that happened after 1945. Not everyone behaved in an exemplary manner. We witnessed a whole flood of denunciations and prosecutions. Maybe someday people will study them and say that Jünger refused to have anything to do with it, he ignored it completely. I could have defended myself, of course, but in such cases, discretion is the better part of valor. The blows miss you, they beat the air.

HERVIER: You have already repeatedly alluded to the position of the anarch, who also plays a major role in your novel *Eumeswil*. How would you define him?

JÜNGER: The best definition is still in terms of the anarch's relationship to the anarchist. As I have told you, the anarchist, contrary to the terrorist, essentially has goals. Like the Russian revolutionaries during the Tsarist era, he wants, say, to blow up monarchs. But most of the time, his efforts backfire rather than helping him, so that he often winds up under the executioner's ax or else kills himself. At times—and this is even more disagreeable—the terrorist who has managed to survive continues to live in his memories; perhaps he even flaunts them. He's like a man who's lost his teeth.

The anarch has no such intentions. His inner strength is far greater. In fact, the anarch's state is the state that each man carries within himself. He embodies the viewpoint of Stirner, the author of *The Unique and its Property*—that is, the anarch is unique. Stirner says: "Nothing gets the better of me." The anarch is really the natural man. He is corrected only by the resistance he comes up against when he wishes to extend his will further than is permitted by the prevailing circumstances. In his ambition to realize himself, he inevitably encounters certain limits; but if they didn't exist, his expansion would be indefinite. That was the fate of, say, the caesars, or the child who does whatever he pleases. So barriers have to be imposed.

The anarch can don any disguise. He remains wherever he feels comfortable; but once a place no longer suits him, he moves on. He can, for instance, work tranquilly behind a counter or in an office. But upon leaving it at night, he plays an entirely different role. Convinced of his own inner independence, he can even show a certain benevolence to the powers that be. He's like Stirner, he's a man who, if necessary, can join a group, form a bond with something concrete; but seldom with ideas. The anarchist is often an idealist; but the anarch, on the contrary, is a pragmatist. He sees what can serve him—him and the common good; but he is closed to ideological excesses. It is in this sense that I define the anarch's position as a completely natural attitude. First of all, there is the man, and then comes his environment. That is the position that I favor at present.

HERVIER: Next to Stirner, Kierkegaard played a part in your reflections on the anarch.

JÜNGER: Yes, but I sense a certain difference. I was very interested in Kierkegaard's novel, *Journal of a Seducer*. Yet in Kierkegaard as in others, in Baader and in Hamann, I stroll about as if I were in the middle of a meadow: sometimes I pick a flower that I particularly like, but I do not identify with the whole.

HERVIER: In earlier times, you tended to stress the opposition between anarchism and nihilism, between scorn and hatred of the father.

JÜNGER: Nihilism is quite distinct from anarchy. In Dostoevsky's *The Idiot*, there is a student named Hippolytus, who very clearly embodies the nihilist, and he eventually commits suicide. Remarkably enough, this Hippolytus believes in an afterlife, but a disquieting afterlife.

HERVIER: In a 1951 essay, you proposed another figure rebelling against the established laws of society, the *Waldgänger* [forest stroller], who saves himself by returning to the forests, according to an ancient Icelandic tradition.

JÜNGER: I agree that I took a further step with the anarch. The latter can turn into a *Waldgänger*, but he can also live tranquilly, sheltered by an obscure job. Despite everything, he's an anarch. Society demands certain forms, certain ruses; but basically, it cannot penetrate a man's innermost core. And if society becomes unbearable, then I become a *Waldgänger*; and of course, I can just as readily be one in a skyscraper. For the symbol of freedom reigns everywhere.

HERVIER: Would you describes Solzhenytsin and other Russian dissidents as *Waldgängers*?

JÜNGER: Yes, but of course, tyranny reaches levels that prevent me from showing myself. If I do so anyhow, I am forced to slip away very quickly; otherwise, I'd be promptly killed. Whereas the anarch. . . . The difference between the anarchist and the anarch also resides in the fact that the anarchist needs society, because he wants to improve it, which the anarch does not seek to do. Solzhenytsin is actually more of an anarchist than an anarch.

HERVIER: Apparently Venator, the hero of *Eumeswil*, is the epitome of the anarch.

JÜNGER: Venator is also a historian. His will is not touched by the historical events, he remains a pure spectator. That is why he has chosen the role of bartender: it gives him the leisure to observe and even slightly despise that whole society of power-wielders. He can recall that the same thing happened under Tiberius, and he enjoys this. That is why I have him undergo a test that is bound to turn out in his favor; for from the viewpoint of voluntary action, he is utterly disinterested. He adapts to a given situation for as long as he likes, obviously.

HERVIER: But he has the chance to live in the proximity of a benevolent and intelligent tyrant. Could he behave in the same way within the framework of a totalitarian state?

JÜNGER: In regard to learning and enriching his experience, he may acquire more in a totalitarian state than under an indulgent man, since greater demands will be made on his intellectual resources.

HERVIER: This position of observer, which is Venator's position, is perfectly suitable to you yourself: to be personally near power, but without participating in it.

JÜNGER: Yes, that seems to be profoundly inscribed in my genes. Thus, I had that position of observer during the time that I found myself in something like the entourage of a proconsul, with the commander-in-chief in Paris. I did my duty conscientiously, but without great passion and without gaining any particular renown. Several times, I had command tasks. In particular, I had to oversee a battalion of auxiliaries, made up of Georgians and representatives of different Russian ethnic groups. When I had to address them through an interpreter, I noticed that I didn't stand in the center, I stood off to the side, and that was where I spoke from. I had thus almost instinctively taken the position of observer. Next comes self-observation, and one is astonished to find oneself in one place rather than another. Perhaps it's also a way of escaping when one gets into a series of overly dangerous situations: one doesn't find oneself directly at the center.

HERVIER: That's an attitude that must be very difficult to maintain in the case of a regime like Hitler's.

JÜNGER: True, but during the Hitler period, I would have felt incapable of plunging headfirst into action. I never rose beyond the rank of captain, and I accomplished nothing outstanding. I took a lot of notes, those in *Parisian Journal*. That was one of my office activities, and I observed people. There are anthills, for instance here, in the woods where I often stroll, where certain very different insects live, namely coleoptera, which occupy special cells and maintain a certain relationship with the ants. My activity at the Raphael was of that ilk, in my small office: German soldiers passed through, officers, judges, but also Jews looking for a little help. And yet this activity had other, very different functions: particularly the function of recording all that.

HERVIER: Doesn't war also constitute a borderline case, in which it is very difficult behaving as an anarch?

JÜNGER: I don't agree. There is a movie that was made by an Argentinean named Cozarinsky, based on my World War II journal, *One Man's War*. The film was also shown in England, and in Germany as *Der Krieg eines Einzelnen*. The filmmaker claims that I waged my war as a private individual; that's partly true, but only partly. When he contacted me, I initially wondered what he was after, and I did not give him permission right away. I wrote to my publisher, Klett-Cotta, asking what this was all about, and he forwarded to me a permission request from the filmmaker. I jotted in the margin: "Obviously a dreamer, but that might be interesting!" And I no longer objected. When the movie was shown on TV, I was at home. My son and my daughter-in-law were visiting, and I told them that I was going to bed, they only had to look at the movie. At breakfast the next morning, they told me: "You did the right thing!" But precisely as an anarch, thanks to the position of anarch that I had adopted. So you see that it was possible. This includes even the lowest areas. If someone says, "I took it easy in my corner," you can be sure that this stems largely from behaving as an anarch.

HERVIER: In your opinion, how should the writer act politically?

JÜNGER: I do not believe that this is the author's task. Naturally, there have always been people who managed to combine literature and politics: I'm thinking of Chateaubriand or even Malraux, who was your Minister of Culture. But I don't know whether that is ultimately good for the literary output. The artistic man may put himself at the center of his painting, his poetry, his sculpture, and the rest is ludicrous. That is why I would not criticize a creator who benefits from a tyrant's favors. He cannot say, "I'm waiting for the tyrant to be overthrown!" For that could take ten years, and by then, his creative powers would be gone. He will therefore try to accommodate himself for better or worse, if he cannot leave the country. The artist's chief responsibility is to his work and not to some sort of political orientation. Egotism is a necessity for him.

HERVIER: So then you're generally hostile to a writer's committing himself politically?

JÜNGER: It's also a question of age: literature and politics diverge to the extent that one is interested, on the one hand, in the world as will, and, on the other hand, in the world as representation. In a young man, the forces issuing from will are still very powerful: remember the sympathy that our classical German writers initially felt with the French Revolution: you enter a situation, but then you're quickly disappointed. You know that Baudelaire originally hailed the Revolution of 1848 as a passionate spectator, but he was rapidly disgusted. And the same thing happened to our [Theodor] Fontane. Young men, whose temperament is still highly active, are unable to resist political temptations, even if it's one of our greatest poets, such as Hölderlin, who is now being drafted for politics. Yet politics plays a very ephemeral and subordinate role in him. Hölderlin expressed himself about politics, for instance, in his poem about the peace of Lunéville, and today they're making such a fuss about it. Upstairs in my library, I have the big edition of Hölderlin: if you gather up the political portion, you won't even have one percent of the total number of pages. His exemplary aspect is of a completely different nature. The writer and, above all, the poet are less ideologues than men capable of uttering exemplary words and creating exemplary characters. Perhaps they have the right to try intervening in politics once: on a major occasion with important consequences, as was the case in the Dreyfus Affair, in which writers played a considerable role. One can then say: "That man was perfect politically." But whether he's a good writer is a completely different story.

IX

LITERATURE

Map and signpost.
On the Marble Cliffs. Heliopolis. Eumeswil.
Writing a novel. The journal.
Mosaic and crystallization.
The function of the poet. The instant of creation.
Timelessness as literary survival.

HERVIER: Yet you did not hesitate to challenge Nazism in *On the Marble Cliffs*, albeit in a veiled form.

JÜNGER: I did indeed, but at the same time, I was called upon by the muse, if I may say so: the political situation had reached its point of poetic concentration, and that was why the work had a political thrust. But the political meaning is not enough: we have to go back to the snakes, the dogs, the holders of power, the martyrs, like Prince Sunmyra, who virtually foreshadows Count Stauffenberg. All the political givens are ephemeral; but what is concealed behind the demonic, the titanic, the mythic remains constant and has an immutable value: *On the Marble Cliffs* preserves its full significance today, in other areas beyond the ones we live in. But at the time, people instantly said: "The Great Forester—that's Goering." Yet it

HERVIER: You personally don't write political books; but they're not apolitical either. Your work does not ignore the world.

JÜNGER: A writer always has a political effect. Even if he moves through regions tempered by the gentleness of friendship, like Rousseau, his influence can be enormous: as strong as that of the Septembrists. However, I prefer the position and attitude of Saint Anthony. I believe it happened in Cairo: he kept watching the Christians passing before him to their martyrdom. He didn't protest, but he did show his cards. When an author exposes his very substance without deliberately trying to exert an influence, the repercussions can be as powerful as if he had launched into a political argument: he provides an example, not an impulse. And the intellectual currents are often highly diverse, highly contradictory. I gladly admit that I prefer drawing a map to playing the role of a signpost.

HERVIER: Yet you did not hesitate to challenge Nazism in *On the* could just as easily have been Stalin; and incidentally, that was how I managed to defend myself. Indeed, when I describe a type, that type can be represented in either the East or the West, more or less forcefully. For me, Stalin resembles the Great Forester far more closely than Goering does. In a dream, one first encounters the type. Then, in reality, one encounters the incarnation of that type in a weakened guise. The reverse is equally possible: by knowing people, personalities, and dreaming about them, one reaches their profound truth. Léon Bloy showed this effectively. People talk about diabolatries and black masses, whereas all they have to do is go and see the corner grocer.

HERVIER: One finds that same general value in *Heliopolis*, even though this novel, in a way, also evokes the atmosphere of the German general staff in Paris, at the Raphael and the Majestic.

JÜNGER: It's a book that should be regarded as a look at the past. It transposes us to an imaginary world, which offers certain characteristics of the count.

HERVIER: However, one cannot help evoking the problem of anti-Semitism here; young Boudour Peri is in a situation similar to that of a Jewish woman in the Third Reich, as we recently said.

JÜNGER: Granted, but Eros also plays its part. For everything concerning anti-Semitism or anti-anti-Semitism, we absolutely have to rely on the reality of behavior and not content ourselves with political orientations or tendencies. An aversion to violence and brutality is certainly innate in some men: they like it or do not like it. And I must say that during the two wars, especially the Second, I made especially sure that nothing of that nature occurred or could occur within the sphere of my activity. It was really difficult to do more than that: I could not take all the suffering of the world upon my shoulders. For that, you have to be gifted with an extremely religious nature.

For the writer, the important thing is to depict what is fundamentally evil, whether it is anti-Semitism or a systematic anti-German spirit. One can have generous judgments, but only on the basis of a dense and concrete description of persons and events, which are not directly linked to the political reality. As Novalis said, "Only that is true which has occurred at no time and in no place." I can also imagine a situation referring to numerous real situations, offering their image, because that image reaches strata common to different historical antagonisms.

HERVIER: The image of democracy proposed by *Eumeswil* is hardly flattering.

JÜNGER: Just what is democracy? People claim to have democracy everywhere, even in countries where it is absolutely non-existent in practice. It's somewhat the same with Truth. Truth is highly praised everywhere: but where do we really encounter it?

Incidentally, in *Eumeswil*, Venator's viewpoint is that of an observer, who keeps aloof of purely political trends. The historian has no right to take sides; in this way, he resembles the tragic actor. For the latter, moral appreciation has only an immanent value. A scoundrel— and this is generally the case—can be described more convincingly than a decent man. The description of paradise is never as successful as that of hell—in Dante, for example, but also in Milton or Klopstock. In these authors, hell is a more fascinating place than the bliss of paradise.

HERVIER: How did you come to write your first novel?

JÜNGER: I believe it is an instinct to be found in every man; I would venture to say that the number of uncompleted novels is far greater than that of the works published. In fact, I know of very few people in my acquaintance who have not wanted to write a novel sooner or later. It's like a mirror: each man's life is a novel, but few men are capable of giving it a universal form, elevating the facts of individual experience to the level of a vaster significance. I don't know whether I've succeeded. In any case, many people recognize themselves in one or another of my characters.

HERVIER: How do you compose your novels? Do you first think of an atmosphere, a plot, or characters?

JÜNGER: I would tend to say that the atmosphere comes first. It's like a tapestry: you work on it, and sometimes the result is altogether different from what you planned. Little by little, it takes on a reality. I have observed, for instance, that it is very hard for me to change a character's name once I have given it to him. That is, the literary personage becomes an individual; which proves that this doesn't come from the man who writes the novel, but from somewhere else, another place: something takes shape, a third reality. At times, it's even a surprise. In the case of *A Dangerous Encounter* I had probably first been thinking of a very different *denouement* for the story. But that's not important; what counts is preserving the atmosphere. You see, I find that in Stendhal, there is always a kind of change in tone towards the end of his novels. Thus, in the final pages of *The Red and the Black*, the hero is guillotined, which strikes me as too false a *denouement*, too fantastic. Stendhal discards the atmosphere that he initially created. And this is true of many novel endings, which are less interesting than the starts. I have the same impression when reading *Bouvard and Pécuchet*: the first scene is marvelous—those two chatterboxes meeting on a bench; but then, the entire progression testifies to an enormous disgust. While in *Salammbo*, the ending is excessively turgid.

HERVIER: So you have the impression that your heroes quickly assume a certain independence from you.

JÜNGER: Certainly, they continue living in the readers, and it is astonishing to see what becomes of them.

HERVIER: And in this phenomenon: do you place great importance on the names: how do you normally choose the names of your characters?

JÜNGER: I often choose proper names by consulting maps; that was how I picked the name Mauclerc in *A Dangerous Encounter*.

HERVIER: Parallel to your novels, which are very important, since you're written four in the last twelve years, you regularly keep a journal, which was published under the lovely title of *Seventy Wanes*.

JÜNGER: That's an hourglass phrase. It's what the sailors shout when the sand has stopped pouring: for instance, "A quarter of an hour has waned!" In me, it is the seventy years that have waned; I began writing it on my birthday, and I am now working on the third volume. In regard to certain literary lives—I am thinking even of Stendhal, and I could also include myself—one has the impression that the journal is more important than the novel. I myself find the journal interesting because it restores time in detail. France has Barrès, Gide, Léautaud, who was a friend of mine—I took great pleasure in translating his text, which he dedicated to the memory of his father.

HERVIER: What relationship do the novels in your *oeuvre* have with the journal?

JÜNGER: You could define a novel or a novella as a crystallization. The journal is more of a mosaic: it is made up of splintered fragments, which can nevertheless be reassembled, yielding a whole that may be more evocative than a novel will be a century from now. Furthermore, my journal is a lot less work: it contains accounts of trips, readings, maxims, daily reflections. Reports on dreams, walks in the country, the growth of plants also play their part: Bourgois was right when he chose flowers to illustrate the cover of the [French] translations of my old war journals.

It's very pleasant for an author. When reading or strolling, he has the leisure to jot something down or not. It's like picking an apple from a tree every day. You don't have to think of the tree in its totality. But if you have your own central point, a totality can emerge, or at least something that makes someone else feel he is dealing with a totality. Sometimes, ten years have gone by without my writing my journal; whereas now, things interest me day by day, and their diversity produces a coherent whole.

HERVIER: And sometimes, a particular crystallization is generated.

JÜNGER: It comes from authentic intuition, which itself exists outside of time. This struck me in regard to *On the Marble Cliffs*, which was triggered by a dream in a single night. But after the flash of intuition, it can take me an entire year to work it out. That's why I often jokingly say to my wife, "Pray to heaven that I don't get an idea!" Because then you become the slave of your own idea, and that's the worst kind of slavery. If a work has to attain a certain rank, it goes back to that initial flash of intuition; then the implementation either succeeds or fails, but in any case, it demands quite a long time. That's why my correspondence and my journal are like the fifth wheel of the carriage for me; those activities are steady, but far less demanding. *Author and Authorship* is in the same category. Reading constantly brings new things; the maxims add up, they don't need a particular arrangement, an organizing concept. In an era dominated by confusion, the maxim, like a small building block, remains something that continues to claim literary value.

HERVIER: In the preface to your war journal, you write: "The function of the poet is one of the highest in the world. When he transmutes a word, minds crowd around him; they have an inkling of the blood offering. The future is thus not only an object of vision; it is evoked and even conjured up."

JÜNGER: It is my supreme conception of the function of the poet, who can transform the world. He, of course, does not profit from it at all, but he can utter the word, and to this extent, he performs a cultic function—he is not a mere entertainer. This intuition is inevitably very rare; but when you read the great classical and romantic poets, you come upon passages that seem to derive from inspiration in a pure state.

HERVIER: In the same passage, you also write: "The effect exerted by an impeccable sentence surpasses by far the pleasure that it bestows by itself."

JÜNGER: That's a central experience. Something lasting is created, which also in and of itself affords pleasure; and this pleasure can be transformed into enthusiasm in very distant places, among unknown readers. There are indeed perfect sentences, but they are extremely rare. However, in Goethe's *Faust*, one often has that feeling: "It is impossible to say this in a better way!"

HERVIER: In regard to your own works, you told me that you never reread them, except to improve their style for new editions.

JÜNGER: Once they're published, I no longer set much store by them. In my opinion, the moment of creation, of composition is the essential. I am convinced, for example, that you know my *oeuvre* better than I do.

HERVIER: And do you know what sort of resonance your various books have in the public?

JÜNGER: You're thinking of their reception. For that, one has to consult the royalty statements that publishers send their authors once or twice a year. As I told you, I recently received a statement, which says that *The Storms of Steel*, even though it first came out in 1920, has been enjoying a lasting interest for over sixty years; and I believe that this is because I relate nothing but facts. I offer no opinion or ideology, I merely recount how the ordinary soldier lived through that war, which was the final war. For since then, there have been no real wars, there are only huge earthquakes, prodigious traffic accidents caused by moments of negligence, inattentiveness, or technological confusion. That which has been thought of as war since the age of Homer no longer exists, except perhaps in Africa. *On the Marble Cliffs* had a more or less equal success. Of course, as any author experiences it, every new publication arouses an initial interest, which subsequently may or may not persist—it all depends. Thus *Author and Authorship* is widely read, as I can tell from my morning mail; and I receive almost more French mail than German mail.

HERVIER: As for posterity, you seem quite pessimistic when you compare literary glory to the glory of having insects named after you.

JÜNGER: You know, my manuscripts are preserved at a bank, in Riedlingen. A while ago, the director of the bank told me that they were absolutely safe, protected against atomic bombs. So I thought that some day, perhaps, there would be no more human beings, and my writings would survive in the depth of their nuclear shelter, even if I haven't deposited anything timeless there. Yet that is my principle: writing has to have a timeless element. Every work ultimately perishes, even Homer will disappear. As the Greeks said, the universe periodically goes up in flames so that it may be resurrected. However, there is something in Homer that has no direct relationship to society: that is what I look for in an author. The longevity of a work is directly dependent on that. Voltaire will not survive as long as some of his contemporaries who possess that element of eternity. Thus, I am convinced that Rousseau will outlive Voltaire, people will continue to be excited by Rousseau, for he has that spark which, for me, symbolizes the eternal values or what are known as the eternal values—the only things that bestow true permanence.

X

FRANCE
A DANGEROUS ENCOUNTER

Celts and Teutons. In the *métro* and in Verdun.
Visiting President Mitterand.
French readings: Verlaine, Rimbaud, Léon Bloy.
Paris friendships. Collaborators.
Drieu la Rochelle. Céline. Paris.
A detective story. Policemen and wrongdoers.
The political system.

HERVIER: Everyone knows about your affection for France, your sensitivity to the specific qualities of Celts and Latins.

JÜNGER: Every European naturally has Celtic blood, and the Teutonic-Celts are a happy combination. I see that expressed particularly clearly in people like Francis I. That dear Henri Plard also obviously has a lot of Flemish elements, considerable affinities with Germany. He plainly speaks German better than many of my compatriots: and he is an excellent French translator. He patently has that Gaul element, but also Latin element, that greater precision. When one has a discussion with a Frenchman, the conversation runs along a more precise line than with someone from Würtemburg. One gains in the precision of words, they are more univocal, the idea comes out more sharply. However, equivocalness is also important in language. . . .

For a long time, I didn't want *The Worker* to be translated [into French]—for one thing because of a purely etymological problem. Arbeiter comes from *arbeo*, a Gothic word, meaning "inheritance." The French word *travailleur* [worker] derives from *tripalium*, a torture instrument. At the very root, there is a risk of fundamental misunderstanding, which the translation could only aggravate.

HERVIER: Volume II of *Seventy Wanes* has just been published in Paris by Gallimard. Are you satisfied with the reception of your work in France?

JÜNGER: Several months after the appearance of Volume I, in November 1984, my wife and I were in Paris, and I was invited to a small luncheon with President Mitterrand. Next, I was scheduled to go to the Senate to give a decoration to an old French military man. We took the *métro*, and a man who was sitting opposite me, dressed in work clothes, stood up, came over, and asked: "Vous êtes Ernst Jünger? [You are Ernst Jünger?]," which I had no reason to deny. He then said: "Je viens de terminer *Soixante-dix s'efface*. Mais où est donc votre femme? [I've just finished *Seventy Wanes*. But where's your wife?]" I ought to say that my wife appears a few times in my book under the name "taurillon," because she was born under the sign of Taurus. The man then asked me: "Où est Madame? [Where is Madame?]" She was sitting behind me, and I pointed to her: he turned towards her, exclaiming "Voilà le taurillon! [There's taurillon!]" I am citing this anecdote simply to show that I feel I am truly being read in Paris. Here is the second volume of the translation: I haven't yet had the time to take a good look at it, just the final pages: you always consult the index in the back to find out what's included; or, if it's one of your own books, to see what the back of the jacket says. On this book, the jacket text seems very well written: so I'm quite hopeful.

HERVIER: How did the meeting with President Mitterand come about?

JÜNGER: I was surprised and delighted that our relations with France have been constantly improving. When we evacuated Paris in 1944, I would scarcely have believed that we could return so soon. But after several years, I was able to go back to Fontainebleau; and my superior and friend, General Speidel, was there as commanding general of the Central European region. Those are astonishing changes, which no one would have dreamed of. Likewise, I would never have thought that some day I would have the opportunity of receiving honors at the garrison of Verdun, in a parade. It was highly comforting for me to witness the meeting of the French and German presidents, in which I had the honor of participating. In Metz, likewise, President Mitterand said a few friendly words to me, and he informed me that a member of his cabinet, a man named Pierre Morel, had translated a collection of my maxims. To make a long story short, the result was that I and my wife were invited to a small luncheon at the Elysée. The dialogue took off easily. Monsieur Mitterand has a background in history and he is also very well-read. I told him that I sometimes feel as if I've landed in the wrong century and not in the right country, that I may even have landed on the wrong planet. He responded: "Au temps de Napoléon, vous seriez sans doute devenu maréchal! [In Napoleon's time, you would probably have become a marshal.]" I wouldn't care to disagree, it is not out of the question: and I replied that marshals were a chapter unto themselves. When I think of Tukhachevsky, when I think of Rommel, I don't have to go back to Ney and Murat. But I do not wish to belabor the point: I would not have had the requisite ambition except during the First World War. I was serving the Prussians then, and one could rise in the ranks only on the basis of seniority. During World War II, it was entirely different, as we can tell from the example of marshals like Rommel and Goering. I might have achieved the same rank, but I had no desire whatsoever. I would much rather have written a good book, a novel. That corresponded some-what to Stendhal's position. He was impressed by many things, but basically, literature was the most important thing in his eyes.

HERVIER: What were your first contacts with French literature? It seems to have had a great influence on you.

JÜNGER: Let us first point out that I was interested not only in French literature, but also in the classical literature of antiquity and, needless to say, that of our German classics. I likewise owe a great deal to the Russians, and more to Dostoevsky than to Tolstoy. I recently noted that Dostoevsky is clearly read less in France than in Germany. My friend Léautaud once told me that this was the literature of luna-cy. But let's get back to France. I started out with, let's say, works of entertainment. My knowledge of French literature goes way back. In high school, I had done an exchange with France when I was fifteen; but before that, I had already read lots of French books in translation. Young boys everywhere prefer deeds and action: in Germany, people were reading Karl May, and in France, Alexandre Dumas. Naturally, *The Count of Monte-Cristo* made a huge impact on me. I don't know whether you agree with me, but I feel that in Victor Hugo's novels there are traces of that slightly facile genre, for certain Frenchman are highly sensitive to this. I was deeply impressed by Hugo's great novels with their escaped convicts and the octopus in *Toilers of the Sea*. But all that was dethroned or put on a higher level when I read Baudelaire as well as Rimbaud. For me, Rimbaud illustrates the fact that a single poem can upset a man's life, transform it from top to bottom. Thus, "The Drunken Boat" had a prodigious impact on me, but I didn't read it until after World War I. I also like Verlaine a great deal, that's my taste for decadent literature. In my opinion, decadence releases forces that would otherwise remain dormant, feeble. A sick man often discovers colors and sounds that are far more different and more subtle than he suspected when he was in good health. That's something that often appears on a death mask, the *lux aeterna*, the great radiance.

HERVIER: And what do you think of the Surrealists?

JÜNGER: At the very top, I would put Max Ernst, with whom I have maintained a correspondence: he is a fundamental Surrealist. But this movement began very early, for instance with people like Lautréamont.

HERVIER: In your war journal, you often quote Léon Bloy, who is a relatively little known author.

JÜNGER: One can wonder why the Germans are so embarrassed in regard to Léon Bloy. I may say that I am German and Protestant; but that man has an access to spirituality, which fascinates me. It's like a tower: at the bottom, there's mud; but at the top, everything becomes eloquent. So I appreciate it only above the cincture.

HERVIER: What German writers would you recommend to the French?

JÜNGER: The French have learned a lot from our Romantics, there is no need to recommend Novalis to them, for they know him very well. Maurice de Guérin, the author of *Centaure*, owes a great deal to Novalis, for whom literature is located beyond reality. The author's task is to elevate the raw givens to a higher level, to spiritualize them.

HERVIER: Your sojourn in Paris at the German general staff enabled you to get to know more of contemporary French literature.

JÜNGER: During World War II, I had a chance to frequent a throng of French writers: Montherlant, Cocteau, Morand. We got together every Thursday in the home of Madame Gould. I also met Resistance members there, like Paulhan, who played an important role in the Resistance. But during that period, we both maintained a discreet silence about that. Our conversations were essentially about literature. I may say—and I thanked my superior, Speidel, who had me transferred to his office in Paris—that this stay had fruitful consequences, which lasted until after the end of hostilities. Friendships such as with Léautaud and especially Jouhandeau have largely survived the war. I like Jouhandeau particularly for his style: he's an exception in our era. Léautaud writes less well, but he is interesting for other reasons. He claimed one should never change a first draft; but I for my part prefer reworking the style.

HERVIER: You also have a great respect for Julien Gracq's style.

JÜNGER: *Lettrines*, for instance, had a deep impact on me.

HERVIER: You also offer impressions of your trip to Japan in the special Gracq issue of *L'Herne*; and in 1965, he paid homage to you in the journal *Antaios*, which you edited together with Mircea Eliade.

JÜNGER: Yes, I had spent a few days in Japan, and I published my first impressions in that tribute in *L'Herne*. In regard to Eliade, we were friends for years, and I feel close to his metaphysical perspectives. He and I edited the journal *Antaios* for ten years. Before the war, he put out the journal *Zalmoxis*; he sent me several issues—and the publisher felt we ought to do a magazine in which "passages" and landscapes would have their place. I went to see him, we reached an agreement, and that was how it came about.

HERVIER: But when you were in Paris during the war, you also met writers who were collaborators, some of whom struck you as worthy of esteem, for example Drieu la Rochelle?

JÜNGER: All his friends considered him an extremely honest man. I was very upset when he committed suicide in a moment of despair. Chardonne, and so many others, managed better and survived without problems. Recently, some young Frenchmen told me that they greatly admired Chardonne, and I replied that I didn't know him. Then I consulted my archives, and I saw that they contained letters from him. Apparently, he even wrote an unpublished book about me. But to get back to Drieu, I was truly pained by his death. He was a man who had suffered greatly. Thus there are people who feel friendship for a certain nation, which was true of many Frenchmen, who felt friendship towards us, which brought them no luck.

HERVIER: On the other hand, Céline aroused your dread.

JÜNGER: With Céline, I had difficulties for which I was not responsible. At the German embassy, in the presence of Epting and Abetz, Céline said very odious things about the measures that the Germans should have taken in Paris, he claimed that we were too indulgent. Since I don't like to write ill of the dead, I encoded his name, calling him Merline in my journal. But I don't quite know what happened: either because of a typesetter during the printing or because of some maneuver by his enemies, Céline's correct name was restored. This happened against my will, and I was very sorry. Incidentally, the huge biography of Céline indicates that I behaved quite properly in this circumstance: I am far from blackening someone, even if he is already black. Céline, of course, was furious; but by then, he was already out of the danger zone, he had resettled in France. Reason got the better of him. He became a classical writer, published in *La Pléiade*, while others were executed, for instance Brasillach, whom I had met several times at the embassy, which he visited because of his functions, his activities. I have just consulted a record of the Brasillach trial. It was rather disgusting to see what the presiding judge told him: "Yes, you went to Weimar with other writers. Didn't you know that at that very same time, such and such a thing was happening very near you? . . ." And he was sentenced to death. It's awful, but it's something that recurs in all eras; in 1779, they were hanging people from the lanterns.

HERVIER: In reading your journal, one feels that even though you met chiefly writers, you were also far more deeply impressed by the painters you visited in their studios, for instance Braque and Picasso.

JÜNGER: That's a very common thing. At present, the works of painters strike me as infinitely more convincing—which doesn't prevent me from maintaining a great interest in prose. And for their part, painters feel a kind of joy at the colored values of my style. I like talking to painters—indeed often. With them, at least, there is always something to see. Whereas with literature. . . . But if painters become too literary, the results aren't good.

HERVIER: You seem plainly less interested in music?

JÜNGER: I am essentially a visual man, although I have a very strong relationship to sounds. This excludes a certain kind of composition that resorts excessively to mathematical representations. The important thing, for me, is natural sounds. French music has an anti-Wagnerism, which pays great attention to natural sounds; I am thinking of such pieces as Debussy's *Jardins sous la pluie*, which goes back to the voices offered by nature. Folksongs can also move me very deeply, and so can Mozart, who, in my opinion, is accessible to anybody: that fully satisfies me. However, the essential things are located beyond the scale of sounds as well as beyond the visible specter. When one is immersed in an ecstatic or transcendental state, the colors, to my mind, are most important when they begin to explode towards barely discernible forms.

HERVIER: You speak about Paris in *Aladdin's Problem*, but in order to say that it has lost its smile.

JÜNGER: Yes, it's a global problem. That which used to be called "le sourire [the smile]" and the joy of serving were highly developed. I returned to that in a story entitled *A Dangerous Encounter*, which is set in Paris in 1890. Here, I invited Jack the Ripper, the celebrated criminal, to give his unusual impression of the Parisian scene. That's not historically accurate, but it's poetic license, the novelist has the right to carry out such transpositions. I took advantage of this right in order to describe Paris before World War I; for the loss of the smile coincides with that war. In 1920, I was sitting on a café terrace in Paris, and an old man from Tonkin or goodness knows where was complaining to me: "Ah! ce n'est pas le Paris d'avant guerre! [Ah! This isn't prewar Paris!]"

HERVIER: In a recent interview, the Czech writer Milan Kundera said more or less: "Paris is still a capital, but the capital of a dying world."

JÜNGER: Yesterday, I spent a long time at the Dôme with Cioran, who told me with his usual pessimism that Paris had lost an awful lot of its old French charm.

HERVIER: Aside from the smile, what else did you appreciate in the Paris of the eighteen-nineties?

JÜNGER: A certain *fin-de-siècle* atmosphere, which we call *Jugendstil*, an atmosphere of decadence, which nevertheless allows a few impressionist gleams to come through.

Furthermore, that was pretty much the incubation period for the Dreyfus Affair. I introduce characters like Sandhecr and Schwartzkoppen, who played an important role in the Dreyfus Affair. That was an era that I consider highly fruitful, in regard to both the decadence and the maturing of very different forces. My stay in Paris certainly counted also for the setting of the plot. The friendships I developed there with writers as well as private individuals enabled me to achieve an overall view of that grandiose city. My little detective story benefited from that.

HERVIER: In your office, you have a picture of the house on Rue du Cherche-Midi where one of the characters in the story supposedly lives.

JÜNGER: I have a special relationship with that street. I had friends there during the war. It was a place of comfort for me: and I expressed my gratitude to that street in *A Dangerous Encounter*. A ruined cuirassier lived there. Balzac says there are streets that resemble fish: the head is very nice, but the tail leaves something to be desired. I really don't know where the head and the tail of Rue du Cherche-Midi are, but one could say that its tail is the military prison, which no longer exists, but which I knew in its time. That was where they incarcerated Dreyfus and then, later on, Stülpnagel, who hanged himself there. He left a note saying: "I am not in a state of mind that allows a Prussian general to appear before a tribunal." And it was that state that I wished to describe more or less in the cuirassier. But one could also say that the tail of that street is higher up, near Montparnasse Terminal. That was likewise a building that I was well acquainted with, and that no longer exists: I live as much in the Paris of the nineteenth century as in that of the twentieth.

HERVIER: How did you hit on the idea of writing a detective story?

JÜNGER: This is not a genre that I am particularly drawn to. I much prefer criminal trials, such as are found in the Pitaval. It is hard to say why you suddenly feel like treating a given subject. Maybe it struck me as amusing twenty years ago, like when my old war buddies said: "Look at him, doing literature!" Nor do I know why, in this very house, I stopped working on this subject halfway through. I haven't a clue as to the reason. Perhaps I was worried that I'd be suspected of turning into a detective-story writer. It can also happen that you read a particularly nasty review, and then you tell yourself: "Why bother writing books that only have unpleasant results!" and you drop the whole thing. Or else you find another subject. At the time, it was the hourglasses: I was preoccupied with the relationship to time, and so I abandoned *A Dangerous Encounter*. The only reason I went back to it was because my wife kept telling me: "I'm curious, I'd like to know how it turns out." But I had lost the thread. The original murderer may have not have been the same as in the final book, I don't know, but it doesn't matter. The earliest critical reactions show me that the story line seems very logical.

HERVIER: What exactly does the title designate?

JÜNGER: This "dangerous encounter" is actually an encounter between two people who are just barely out of adolescence, two young people who are still unaware of the rules of the game and have not yet mastered either the technique or the psychology of love; and the outcome can only be bad. However, the "dangerous encounter" properly speaking takes place between a man whom I call Ducasse and the young hero. It is Ducasse who precipitates the drama, with his plan to wreak vengeance on mankind; unfortunately, he succeeds all too well.

HERVIER: This Ducasse has actually fallen even lower than the cuirassier in his downfall.

JÜNGER: Yes, Ducasse embodies a certain form of downfall. His ambition was to revive once again the society of the eighteenth century. But for him, this is possible only in a purely technical way, for neither the outer circumstances nor the internal equilibrium of society have the appropriate capacity. He has arrived in an era where there are neither masters nor servants, and he preserves the old demands.

HERVIER: Doesn't this narrative contain a sort of meditation on the relationship between order and criminality within the framework of a policed society?

JÜNGER: Actually, everything is ambivalent: this is a universal law that goes far beyond the precise case of the criminal and the policeman, to the extent that everything has its bright side and its dark side; and the latter is indispensable. The physician, too, must have a proper relationship to illness; otherwise, he can't heal. We've talked about the snake: its venom has both therapeutic power and deadly effects, and the same applies in this case. Incidentally, this kinship is well known: if you immerse yourself in a criminal trial, you have a very hard time distinguishing between the activity of the police and that of the criminal. They join together in the person of the honorable correspondent, the "stool pigeon," as he is called: he is half policeman and half criminal. He has to have free access to the underworld. Those are two overlapping activities.

Very often, they mingle so disturbingly that you can't tell them apart. I'm thinking of, say, the burning of the Reichstag. Even today, no one knows what really happened. This is due to the ambivalence of facts in general, in which the criminal element and the police element are so entangled that any distinction has become impossible.

HERVIER: You once used an anecdote to illustrate the relationship between the Prussian system and the British system. In a hotel, where the guests are arguing and are about to come to blows, the Prussian can't stand the disorder and he tries to intervene immediately: but to no avail. The Englishman, on the contrary, allows things to go on. It is only when the situation becomes truly serious that he gathers the less intoxicated and more reasonable guests and, with their help, he vigorously restores order.

JÜNGER: Every political situation presumes a certain amount of disorder. Even under a more or less passable government, the man who holds the cross always blesses himself first, as they say. There are even situations in which a certain amount of corruption ensures the smooth functioning of things: a machine that runs without oil wears out a lot faster. I don't mean to praise corruption, but nothing ever operates in a purely mathematical way. We experience this daily.

XI

ALADDIN'S PROBLEM

The cult of the dead and contemporary magic.
Priests and the sacred.
Cancer and the atomic bomb.
Real health. East Germany.
Nietzsche. Death and immortality.

HERVIER: Your piece of fiction that preceded *A Dangerous Encounter* was titled *Aladdin's Problem*. What precisely is this problem? And why Aladdin?

JÜNGER: That is what I would term a classical question. Personally, I find the problem quite simple. But it frequently happens that an author finds his own ideas simple because he feels at home, while others are unable to get their bearings. In fact, Aladdin's problem is twofold. First of all, culture is declining. How was culture born? It was born with the cult of the dead, with the religious worship of ancestors; that began with the pyramids and with the tumuli built by prehistoric men, with their caves and grottoes. All these things are vanishing and are even extinct. I focused on these burial issues because I regard the disappearance of ancestor worship as a characteristic of present-day decadence. When I stroll through a cemetery, I am struck by the sadness, which is aroused not by the unfortunate deceased, but by the dreadfully uniform way in which people think about them.

Thus the original idea for *Aladdin* probably came to me when I visited a totally abandoned cemetery in New York. Everything was impeccably clean and well kept, but I sensed that noboby ever came there. Only the florist delivery men still show up on fixed dates to deliver bouquets. Incidentally, there is a frightful story by Maugham or an author of that ilk [Evelyn Waugh—Translator's note]: *The Loved One*. It describes the way in which people now embellish the dead while trying to get rid of them as fast as possible. For instance, one can have the deceased's pipe inserted into his mouth, or put makeup on his face. This description is both fascinating and consternating at once.

When a man is dead, people believe that he is gone forever. According to that logic, there can be no art. For art offers more than pure presence, it offers transcendence. If the cult of the dead were to reappear, it would be a sign that culture can take root again. That is the idea of the narrator who accidentally comes into contact with that universe because his uncle owns a funeral home.

HERVIER: But it's a huge establishment. Isn't that a mere business rather than a real worship of the dead.

JÜNGER: It's always like that. Transcendence also implies the banality of immanence. That, *entre nous*, is the great concern of priests. It was already so in Egypt: all the people who embalmed mummies and who worked in quarries to build the pyramids. Those are two faces of one and the same thing. And in our civilization, it has to be manifested in the same way. Or rather, it ought to, because now it is a fiction.

In the second place, we are in the situation of possessing a formidable power. We extract things from the earth non-stop; oil, uranium, etc. Our situation resembles that of Aladdin. He is a young man who has received an instrument from a magician—a miraculous lamp with an enormous power. All he has to do is rub it, and a powerful genie appears, who gets him anything he wants. He can ask for a harem or construct a palace in a single night. We have the same capability. Aladdin's lamp is made of terracotta or copper. Our lamp also comes from the earth, but it is made of uranium. If we rub it, we don't get light, we get more than light: we get monstrous forces. And what does Aladdin draw from his lamp? He has palaces built, he does everything that a child's mind could wish for. That, incidentally, is the charm of the tale. But ultimately, he leads a mediocre life, the kind every mediocre man dreams about: he leads the life of a little despot, whereas he could have gained mastery of the whole world, from Mauritania to China. And then, he does a lot of stupid things; one day, he loses his lamp, and the magician regains his power.

The parallel strikes me as highly fruitful, for we are in exactly the same situation. Monstrous energies come to us, and what do we do with them? Instead of building a magnificent world and great utopias where, for instance, no one would have to work—we don't even consider it, we use our lamp to stockpile nuclear bombs. The genies we conjure up are not good ones: we go east and west, and we may be dashing towards our doom.

Thus the problem would be as follows: 1. transcendence; 2. the ability to intelligently administer the power that breaks in on us.

HERVIER: What worries me is the similarity between the large-scale capitalist Zapparoni in *The Glass Bees* and the other capitalist, Jersson, in *Aladdin's Problem*.

JÜNGER: Yes, but he is raised to a higher power. The great capitalists do a golden business with funerals, but that says nothing against transcendence. That is the secret of priests, Levites. As for Uncle Fridolin, he is a good man, who is surprised by the events. Once things become realities, they are no longer interesting. That is an effect of technology in general. When I was a boy, there was a great debate about whether it was possible to fly in something heavier than air. Peopled argued about it. And what happened? The two houses I inhabited in Hanover were destroyed by bombs. The materialization of a thing brings banalization and disappointment. When people talked about flying in the air, they pictured something very different. We have realized something that was a fantasy dream for our fathers. Like eagles, we have soared up towards the cosmos. And the same disappointment is found in *Aladdin*. Perhaps man will ultimately fall ill because of his disappointment. But there is nevertheless a gleam of hope. The return of the gods is not impossible, it is even being timidly heralded.

HERVIER: At the start of *Aladdin*, you talk about sickness, particularly cancer.

JÜNGER: Yes, that is the great, widespread fear among people today, the fear of the next war and the fear of illness. It is manifested at the end of each millennium. It's a millenarian fear; as at the birth of Christ and towards the year 1000, when people believed that Paraclete was about to come back. That's what's happening today. But in older times, it was part of religion, whereas today, it stems purely from the machine, for we no longer live in the age of the gods, we live in the age of the titans and giants.

HERVIER: In *Aladdin*, you even seem to suggest that people die simply because they're afraid—afraid of cancer or the atomic bomb.

JÜNGER: Yes, that's perfectly true, and it's obvious chiefly in heart disease. Apparently, the central system is attacked, and this is accompanied by a kind of anxiety that aggravates the case. But it also involves a relationship to transcendence: if my relationship with it is harmonious, death can only bring me a higher state. Which doesn't mean I have to be in any hurry. . . . That is why the various religions are indispensable, including that which concerns man's real health. Real health has nothing to do with ailments of the body. A man may be struck by a deadly illness and still be in unfailingly good health, while another may be in dazzling health, even though his prognosis is hopeless.

HERVIER: It's that aspiration to get beyond sheer physiology that probably explains the confessor role played by psychoanalysts in America.

JÜNGER: It's a kind of surrogate. For us, too, the sects are taking off. This is a sign that the churches are no longer really playing their part.

HERVIER: What about the hope for the arrival of extraterrestrials?

JÜNGER: Yes, there are people who speak about the return of the gods and go to Mexico to look for their traces. All this adds a great deal of passion to opinion. But it's always the unexpected that occurs: Christ came from a very obscure milieu!

HERVIER: At the end of your book, you talk about Phares: this character already appeared as a sort of archangel at the end of *Heliopolis*.

JÜNGER: That's right, in the last chapter. Everyone has a certain number of key images. Phares-Seraph is an anagram: the Seraphim. He is a figure who brings hope, but very vaguely. One shouldn't be too precise in this area.

HERVIER: *Aladdin* is also a book about East Germany.

JÜNGER: I've never been there, but I have no trouble imagining it. It's the same everywhere. A certain state of poverty, but in which the Prussian ideal is preserved better than in Western consumer society. The figure of the Worker is more sharply embodied in the Kremlin than in us. We live in a bourgeois world. I am not talking about economy: for the figure of the Worker, economy is quite secondary; power is first and foremost. And if we look at the world, the empires that divide it up, we notice that this power is far more distinct in the East than in the West. Naturally, man suffers from the rigorous discipline. But he can always tell himself: "Fine, if that's the way it is, I'll participate; someone like me always takes top place, no matter what the regime may be. I only have to use the right formulas and become the master."

HERVIER: Is it primarily power that interests you in the Prussian ideal of East Germany?

JÜNGER: Yes, but even more the practical character, the rejection of the figurative. It's like the bees in the organization of the hive. They have a state order that's more perfect than ours, because there, everything takes place on the level of facts. If, in the course of evolution, we proved to be merely a secondary branch, the vertebrates—all vertebrates—might disappear. But the insects, the Coronado beetles, for example, can, proportionately, endure a thousand times more radioactivity than we can. So long periods of evolution could be spared; but these are purely speculative thoughts, which do not go beyond the framework of time.

HERVIER: Isn't that a hypothesis on the will of the earth, which you have already spoken about?

JÜNGER: As Nietzsche says, the worst thing is to doubt the will of the earth. You worked on the Colli and Montinari edition of Nietzsche, which I also use, and I am amazed that his later texts, which reveal his madness, still contain astounding images.

HERVIER: The hero of *Aladdin* is forced to submit to the system in order to scale the ladder; isn't the anarch's position more difficult for him in East Germany, than for the hero of *Eumeswil*, who inhabits a laxer world?

JÜNGER: The position of the anarch is possible anywhere. He wants to live for himself, and naturally, as Stirner says, he has to enter society, but without trying to arouse attention—above all, without getting involved in politics, which could only cause him trouble. The hero of *Aladdin* enters the ruling spheres without accepting the least ideological commitment. On the contrary, without ideology, one more effectively represents the rational structure.

HERVIER: Yet in the conversation with his Polish friend, he says: "One must take sides"; whereas his friend feels that one can live by keeping one's distance.

JÜNGER: Those are traces of their national backgrounds; that is how they talk about Pomerania. But they promptly drop the subject.

HERVIER: In *Aladdin*, there is also a relationship that is very sketchy—the relationship between the hero and his wife. It reminds me of the one between Captain Richard and his wife in *The Glass Bees*. In both cases, we have a man lost in a city where he is looking for work.

JÜNGER: Yes, his wife is his only mainstay. But when he is in bed at night, they think they could always remain like this; they would have to be in a pyramid, and they would wake up every hundred years. That is precisely the security embodied by the earth, and the wife as such represents the earth. It is not a purely rational relationship; eroticism is also at the basis of all that.

HERVIER: You also suggest that his relationship to his wife is deteriorating. One is reminded of the parable of Ortner in *Heliopolis*: he's sold his soul, and he loses the love of his spouse.

JÜNGER: Yes, his wife feels that he is losing his transcendence, that he is becoming purely a businessman.

HERVIER: In this book, you seem very alive to the problem of aging and death.

JÜNGER: Oh? I don't know whether it's a sign of growing old, but it didn't really strike me.

HERVIER: At the end of *Eumeswil*, there is the trip to the forests with the tyrant, whom you call the Condor: isn't that a trip towards death?

JÜNGER: Yes, the forest is a symbol of life and death. The great symbols are ambivalent, aren't they? That's a bit paradoxical. Death is something that lots of people envisage with fear. I don't think that's true in my case; but I do think that paradise is not enough.

HERVIER: Yet you were speaking of a kind of immortality.

JÜNGER: Yes. The Christian vision stems from an imperfect situation, which it wishes to make absolutely perfect. Such a vision suddenly invents hell, and it is hard for me to enjoy paradise on earth if I risk stewing in hell. Schopenhauer said a lot of excellent things about that. But I didn't realize I was dwelling on it.

XII

VISIONS OF THE FUTURE

A certain gloominess.
The world state. The regions.
The agony of the idea of the nation.
The nuclear risk. Explosion and compression.
A magic time. Aldous Huxley.
The obsolete utopias.
The Age of John and the Age of Aquarius.
An ultimate optimism.

HERVIER: If I focus on the two utopias of your great novels *Heliopolis* and *Eumeswil*—1949 and 1977 respectively—it seems that your view of the world has definitely grown more somber.

JÜNGER: Yes, but I would like to say that I do not want this to be interpreted as a prophecy about the future. At the moment, there is a portion that involves everything that Nietzsche says about his last man. For me, the last man is, above all, a phantom: man living amid comfort, as depicted in Nietzsche's *Zarathustra*, is only the before-last, and another will soon emerge. This is the kind of thought that comes to mind at twilight, and that is then pondered. But *Eumeswil* does not boil down to that. As for the period of *Passage of the Line*, which, Heidegger says, should have posted the problems differently, I was playing an optimistic game. This doesn't mean that I'm contradicting myself, I am simply revealing facts that contradict one another. This an entirely different matter.

Above all, I want to avoid being frozen in a static image. Perhaps I'll have different notions tomorrow. Despite everything, the course of thinking remains highly instructive: it's like a courtroom trial: "What? Was that your intention? What would have happened if such and such a thing . . . etc." Total decadence is certainly possible. But it is still indispensable for man to intervene and make use of his freedom. He can always change everything. Take the Thirty Year's War, for instance: the German language was deteriorating. And then along came men like Opitz and, much later, Klopstock. I would say the same thing about the linguistic degradation peculiar to our era.

HERVIER: Do you feel that the Americanization of Europe and the invasion of its languages by English share some of the responsibility?

JÜNGER: Léautaud, for example, would have preferred a German victory to an American one, for cultural reasons.

But certain facts point in the opposite direction. There are excellent novelists in America, better ones than here: Hemingway, Faulkner, and so many others. Their works are valuable for their subjects as much as for the great quality of their style. Even if [our] language loses a great deal of syntactical richness through contact with English, we may nevertheless wonder why it is that the British have such a remarkable poetry.

HERVIER: The division of Germany has taken us a long way from the "world state" which you used to dream about. How do you feel about it today?

JÜNGER: I once also wrote a utopian work about peace. The idea is precisely that of today's united Europe. But you can see the present situation in Brussels and Strasbourg; they argue about butter, milk, eggs, or potatoes, yet they never talk about a common government or the elimination of borders. It's absurd: countries that you can fly across in less than five minutes want to keep their borders! It's primitive and even reactionary; and in this respect, I'm disappointed. What can be the future of the world state if a handful of Europeans can't even reach an agreement? Everything is global, the telegraph as well as air links, but we still don't have a world government. That's exactly Aladdin's problem, which is no mere fiction. We seem to be regressing more and more instead of advancing. That's a worldwide phenomenon: thoughts move at a different speed than actual events. Long ago, Kant already wrote about universal peace, but we are as far from that goal as ever.

HERVIER: So we are not dealing with a progressive or circular movement of history; our present situation and the fact that the world state is unable to emerge—are those things sheer chance?

JÜNGER: Something has to happen. Perhaps a catastrophe. For the moment, it remains diffuse from the absolute viewpoint of the spiritual. But materially, it has an implacable logic.

HERVIER: You also feel that the regions will be gaining importance. You know how difficult that would be in France, given the importance of the Paris centralization. You likewise know the current problem of Corsica, which, incidentally, you've visited several times.

JÜNGER: If ever the world state is to come about, or at least the preliminary stage of a united Europe, the nations, such as they have formed after 1789, have to merge together little by little: I mean the fatherlands. On the other hand, the regions—Normandy, Cher, Marseilles, etc.—what I call the motherlands, will become more and more important. Centralism will diminish on this level, and it will shift to utterly enormous entities. But is there a way of translating the word *Heimat* [homeland] into French?

HERVIER: The words that you've just used are hard to render into French: only the word *Vaterland* [fatherland] is well translated by the word *patrie*. We have no word for *Mutterland* [motherland] or *Heimat*, which refers to the house, the home.

JÜNGER: In, any case, we have to get away from the concept of the nation as it was developed by the French Revolution. The consequences were very baleful. The Germans, in turn, took it over. An empire is a lot better. In an empire, everyone can speak whatever language he wishes—Polish or Yiddish—one's mother tongue, whatever it may be. But in a nation state, everyone has to speak the same language, etc. This would be possible in a world state that was not based on a single nation. Small groups would have an entirely different existence there. This is my dearest wish. No army would be needed. The atomic bomb would be controlled on a global level; we would only have to transform nuclear energy into pure energy. Even the man in the street understands that, but governments seem totally unaware of it.

HERVIER: How do you feel about the peace movement in Germany

JÜNGER: It's a fad. Who doesn't want peace? But once a political problem emerges, then so does militarism. It's paradoxical. But it's not my concern.

HERVIER: Still, you're very aware of the risk of a nuclear disaster.

JÜNGER: The fact that today the weight of the world rests on the shoulders of two partners inevitably causes a kind of movement of balance in armaments: one partner arms himself, the other has to take that into account, and he arms himself too. It's like a set of scales: you keep loading up both sides, and you risk breaking the arm of the scale. You're sitting right where [Alberto] Moravia was sitting a few months ago. He wanted to ask me questions about the atomic bomb, and all I could answer was that I consider what's known as the balance of power more disastrous. My feeling is that everything ought to be in one hand. Whose? East or West, I don't care; but actually, there would no longer be any East or West. People could then think about governing sensibly and making economic use of the monstrous power at our disposal. We ought to think about it. Instead, we keep stockpiling more and more explosive material. The Americans may have lost their chance. They had the monopoly at a certain point; they should have consolidated their monopoly and handed it over to a kind of world committee. Had they done so, our present situation would be totally different. Now it's possible for what's known as a star war to break out,—that's the problem of the day. It would be just as possible to imagine a pure intellectual confrontation and an exchange of intellectual power, as in chess. During the Renaissance, that kind of phenomenon took place. Cavalry regiments were so expensive that the rulers didn't really want to destroy them in battle: each regiment tried to occupy as favorable a position as possible, and the opponent gave in. Such a solution is not truly inconceivable; the fact that physicists and scientists, the great incarnations of the figure of the Worker, find ways of making such a conflict absurd. Today, it's absurd, but, in a certain degree, mechanically absurd. It would be an intellectual achievement to drive the absurd so far that such an encounter could no longer take place. People would say: "We'd rather get along." The only solution is the world state. Technologically, it's already here, but politics always lags behind the technological evolution.

HERVIER: Does that mean that the current hazards, including those involving the destruction of the environment, are—as you analyzed it in 1932—linked to the fact that we are entering an era dominated by the figure of the Worker?

JÜNGER: Naturally, those phenomena are part of the negative consequences of a world of titans, which produces a surplus of forces that can lead to catastrophes. The Worker and the figure of the Worker are in a phase of titanism; this is the era in which we have to live. I was recently invited to the Ministry of Defense, and there, from the top of a skyscraper, you can gaze down at other people, who look very tiny. You feel as if you were in a Piranese nightmare. I felt the same malaise at the Centre Pompidou, with its basement, where security agents are scared that someone might set off a bomb. But perhaps the next century will bring us other kinds of enlightenment. If I had to stick to purely technological considerations, I would say that we are currently living in a era in which scattering plays a major role; for example, in nuclear explosions. Nothing prevents us from thinking that we are in an explosive stage, but that a contraction remains possible. We are witnessing attempts at triggering a new fusion of the atom, which could liberate enormous energies for peace. In purely symbolic terms, this could refer to the idea that a certain spiritualization of the world can be manifested according to a healthy orientation. We are now convinced that the world began with an initial explosion, a Big Bang. But every explosion also has its compression, every heartbeat has its systole and its diastole. We could perhaps reach a new spiritual age with different formulations, and an entirely different use of technology: the transformation of technology into pure magic—for instance, the transformation of the telegraph into telepathy, and things of that nature, like a new method of mastering gravity, or whatever! There are so many things in the offing.

HERVIER: In *Seventy Wanes*, you write: "Technology can assume a magical tendency, it can become spiritual or turn to stone, according to the model of animal gregariousness, as Huxley described it."

JÜNGER: It's possible that a magical time is coming. The whole of technology would be transformed: technology as we know it would become purely a preliminary stage, yielding to silent and pleasant devices that would be run by only a small number of men. An embryo, for example, has lungs before it actually needs them; it's a preliminary phase that makes birth possible, a kind of anticipatory programming as the current phrase goes, for the moment when the baby is born; once the umbilical cord is cut, the baby can take its first breath of air. So it can't be ruled out that the figure of the Worker may be in an embryonic state at this moment; and perhaps we'll get to see him in an entirely different state. However, this can't come about without the help of man on the one hand and without transcendental influences on the other hand—what Heidegger designates as "the gods."

HERVIER: That's what you wrote me: one has to knock on the door, but it also has to yield on the other side.

JÜNGER: That's true purely in physical terms.

HERVIER: But there's also the other term of the alternative. You've just said that Nietzsche's last man was merely the next-to-last.

JÜNGER: Since you've read *Eumeswil*, you must have noticed that in my opinion the last man has already come; but behind that last man, we can just barely discern the ultimate man, who is nothing but a phantom. That's a somber vision of the future, it's sort of what will survive after an atomic conflict.

HERVIER: Shouldn't we fear, very concretely, that biology may some day mass-produce human beings, the way we now manufacture cars and washing machines?

JÜNGER: That was what Aldous Huxley feared in *Brave New World*, which depicts that termite state quite perfectly. It's an entirely immanent world; at sixty years of age, you're at the end of your tether, the best solution is suicide. That's one of the dangers. And even here, when I see your tape recorder: in the past, this apparatus would have been completely useless. Recording is one more way of approaching the termite state. The results cannot possibly be changed. If we had decided to speak without a tape recorder, our words could have been constantly revised; whereas here, everything is recorded once and for all, as in an anthill.

However, I have the impression that biology and science in general have reached a post-Huxleyian stage. It's an astonishing development to see that the utopias—for instance, those of Jules Verne—have already been largely rendered obsolete by the progress of our technology. If you recall *Around the World in Eighty Days*, it's now laughable: you can get around the world in eighty hours! And the trip to the moon! In Jules Verne, they take off in an enormous shell that is drawn by means of a powder charge. Nowadays, the solution is a lot more astute. I once said to my father: "We may eventually fly to the moon!" He replied: "I don't think it's possible!" Physicists were doing a tremendous job, and my father imagined that extraordinary forces could be released; but the idea of a trip to the moon struck him as too fantastic. Meanwhile, probes have been sent to Venus, and they have passed within a short distance of Uranus. We can easily build devices that can escape the earth's gravitational pull. So the utopias have been surpassed: but it is important to note that at a certain time, they tended to be pessimistic. Once, they were optimistic, from Campanella's *Sun City* to Jules Verne; but then, pessimism began to take the upper hand. Huxley is a fine example; but I remember that when I was a boy, I read a utopian story about the Martians invading us, and the results were terrible: those Martians found us to be awfully primitive; and since then, utopias have taken a disastrous turn. But perhaps something of that ilk occurs every thousand years. Before the year one thousand, people were extremely pessimistic, they expected large-scale destruction; but nowadays, this pessimism has taken on a technological coloring. Things will probably develop very differently from what we fear.

HERVIER: In an earlier conversation, you told me that you were counting on subsequent generations to resolve those still unknown problems.

JÜNGER: I've observed that each generation brings the means necessary for its existence, and that it realizes itself in a way that no one would have dared to envision, much less dream. I have the feeling that these young people already have a very precise idea of what they want. This idea may strike us as absurd, and it may not be suitable for us; but they will make their way just like us, and they may even have a less difficult time of it. I can only wish them bon voyage.

HERVIER: What place can we hope that the cultured man will have within this new civilization?

JÜNGER: The artistic man has always occupied a place that he himself had to create by means of a hard struggle. He is tolerated to some extent. You probably know Schiller's poem in which Zeus has already distributed all the goods of the earth and can only tell the poet that his place is next to him, and that it will be his as often as he wishes. That is how we must think today. Indeed, nothing very new happens to the artistic man. Basically, *homo technicus* is his enemy; I realize this when I am lost in thought, and a jet fighter zooms past, or even a simple lawn mower. I can then see where my enemy is!

HERVIER: In any case, you expect great changes for the rest of humanity.

JÜNGER: We have to admit that cycles which are far more important than purely historical cycles are now returning. The tide is extremely high whenever the moon and the sun are in the same line; and for us, it is the historical event: the return to caesarism and, furthermore, a tacking about, a phase of which we are ignorant, and which can therefore bring the return of situations outside the science of history. Perhaps astrologers, astronomers, and prophets can tell us more about it than someone like myself.

HERVIER: What can we await astrologically from Aquarius?

JÜNGER: Astrologers foresee the coming of the Age of Aquarius; and certain Christian currents believe in the advent of a Johannine Era. Both those conceptions of the world are optimistic and rather harmonious. The Age of the Father is followed by the Age of the Son, always at intervals of a thousand years; and ultimately comes the Age of the Holy Spirit. And for astrologers, it's Aquarius, a sphere, a state of extreme spiritualization. First, we see only the reverse side: the ancient values are assaulted, they become unreliable. We can only hope that this spiritualization will continue to progress. But for the moment, we are going through an era of transition, of *chiaroscuro*, in which sharply defined phenomena are few and far between. The ancient values no longer obtain, and the new ones have not yet been imposed. It is a world in the shade.

You can observe a ubiquitous ambivalence of opinions. Some people maintain one thing, others the exact opposite: the two sides cancel each other out, even on the highest level, in the relations between East and West, between the twentieth and the twenty-first centuries. On this point, I like to quote an old Russian chronicle, which said about some Mongolian or Tartar invasions: "And this unbearable situation lasted for four hundred years!" Let us hope that the transitional period is ending and that the start of the next millennium will bring agreeable conditions. For my part, I sense that the twenty-first century will be better than the twentieth.

HERVIER: So your prognosis for the future is confident?

JÜNGER: We have to be very prudent in this area. Schleiermacher loves the term "ultimately." I would like to say to you that "ultimately" my prognosis is favorable, which does not mean that dreadful situations might not arise now and then. As for the immediate future, my optimism is not very solid. I'm no Christian, but a good Christian has no reason to worry. For the prophets: once we have crossed all the deserts, something new will eventually transpire. In all great visions, like those in the *Edda*, in the visions of divinity, the titans revolt against the gods, and the gods initially lose; but in the end, they return. There are fewer and fewer Christians. They are greatly concerned with all the grave material dangers we are now threatened with; whereas, above all, they ought to nourish a great hope. In the hymns of the good era, this is expressed marvelously:

> I perceived your splendor, Lord, from afar,
> I would like to link heart to it in advance,
> And, Sublime Creator, I would so much like
> To give you the gift of my negligible life.

Those were still Christians who lived their faith in the full metaphysical sense of the word. That mentality is extremely rare today. People are cut off from transcendence, transcendence is vanishing. But if someone somehow still preserves this relationship to transcendence, he is "ultimately" safe from fear. He can have the feeling of participation, he can tell himself that horrible things are happening, but that behind them a great light is dawning.

CHRONOLOGY

1895   At twelve noon on March 29, Ernst Jünger is born in Heidelberg. He is an Aries with Cancer rising. His mother, nee Lampl, is from Franconia, his father, Ernst, from Lower Saxony. As a pharmacist and chemist, the father achieves a very solid comfort, if not wealth. Ernst Jünger is the eldest of seven children, two of whom die young; the only ones to reach adulthood are a sister and three brothers, of whom the most renowned is Friedrich Georg, a writer, poet, and philosopher, whose work deserves greater recognition abroad.

Ernst spends most of his childhood and adolescence in Hanover, where his parents have relocated after his birth. The family moves several times before settling in a beautiful suburban villa near a lake. But Ernst also attends boarding school in Hanover and Brunswick from 1905 to 1907. He is a wool-gatherer, and his report cards point out his inattentiveness: "I had developed a kind of aloof indifference, which allowed me to be tied to reality only by means of an invisible thread, like that of the spider." He is a passionate reader and, with his brother Friedrich Georg, he inhabits a romantic and exalted universe. One spring, the two boys go back-packing for a week in the country, where Ernst is delighted with the tramps they run into. But he soon dreams of a greater exoticism.

1913   Flight to the French Foreign Legion, which takes him to Oran and Sido-Bel-Abbes. Five weeks later, his father manages to get him repatriated. He subsequently recounts his adventure, slightly transposed, in *African Games* (1936). His father promises not to oppose the son's love of adventure and agrees to find him a place in a Kilimanjaro trek, on condition that he complete high school. Ernst Jünger eventually uses his experiences at the Guildemeister Institute in the novel *The Slingshot* (1973), which evokes that atmosphere.

1914   In August, Jünger passes his final exams in an emergency session and volunteers for the army. From 1914 to 1918, he fights on the French front. He is wounded fourteen times and receives the highest German decoration, the Pour le Mérite, which was created by Frederic II; today, Jünger is the only surviving bearer of that medal. He finishes the war as a lieutenant in the shock troops.

1919   In a time when many of his comrades, young officers, fight in the volunteer corps [*Freikorps*], Jünger remains in the army, where he works on a booklet of tactical rules for the infantry.

1920   He publishes at his own expense his first book, *The Storms of Steel*, which brings him immediate renown.

At the time of the Kapp Putsch, Jünger shows little revolutionary enthusiasm. Drawn by the problems of the military infirmary in Hanover, where he was treated for a cold, he unhesitatingly agrees with his superior, Major von Stülpnagel, who insists, above all, on respecting order. Having to carry out his responsibilities as an officer during the demonstrations, Jünger tries to avoid confrontations, and he is pleased, above all, that he has helped a few strollers who accidentally wandered into the crowd as it was about to riot.

1923   He leaves the army and begins studying zoology at the University of Leipzig. Released from his military duties, he takes up contact with Rossbach, a leader of the voluntary corps, in order to represent the movement in Saxony. But he is soon disappointed by the comings and goings of dubious figures, who primarily try to borrow money from him; he asks to be relieved of his duties.

1925   He continues his zoology studies in Naples. He marries Gretha von Jeinsen. Jünger moves to Leipzig, where he lives as a free-lance writer. That year, he publishes his first articles as a political journalist in *Die Standarte*, an extremist supplement to the journal of the Steel Helmets, the largest German veterans' organization.

1926   Birth of his son Ernst.

1927   Relocation to Berlin. Jünger lives in fairly straitened circumstances. This is the great period of his activity as a political polemicist. Linked to national-revolutionary circles and in particular to the "National Bolshevist" Niekisch (whom Hitler arrested in 1937 and sent to a concentration camp, where he remained until 1945, half blind and paralyzed), Jünger writes not only for *Die Standarte*, but also for other periodicals, some of which are underground, e.g., *Arminius, Der Vormarsch* [*The Forward March*], *Widerstand* [*Resistance*], etc. This activity, while intense from 1928 to 1930, gradually recedes until his final articles in 1932.

      Jünger meets many people: Ernst von Solomon, Otto Strasser, Bertolt Brecht, Arnolt Bronnen, Erich Mühsam, Ernst Toller; he is especially close to Carl Schmitt, Valeriu Marcu, Alfred Kubin, and the publisher Ernst Rowohlt.

1929   Publication of the first part of *The Adventurous Heart*. Trip to Sicily. Jünger, who goes on numerous and sometimes lengthy trips once he has the wherewithal, travels to the Balearic Islands (1932), Dalmatia (1933), Norway (1935), Brazil and the Canary Islands (1936); not to mention trips to Paris, such as the one on which he meets Gide in 1937.

1931   Goebbels vainly tries to draw him to the Nazi Party.

1932   *Der Arbeiter* [*The Worker*].

1933   Jünger refuses to join the German Academy of Writers, which is dominated by the Nazis. The authorities search his home, trying to find letters from Mühsam, an anarchist. In December, Jünger leaves Berlin and withdraws to the small town of Goslar.

1934   He writes a letter of protest to the *Völkischer Beobachter*, the organ of the Nazi Party, which has published an excerpt from *The Adventurous Heart*, without his permission and without indicating the source, thereby making him seem a contributor to the newspaper. Birth of his son Alexander (now a physician in Berlin and the father of two children).

1936   Relocation to Überlingen, on the shores of Lake Constance.

1938   Voyages to Rhodesia, during which he has a visionary dream, in which Hitler appears to him in the midst of his gang.

1939   Relocation to Kirchhorst, near Hanover. Completion of *On the Marble Cliffs*, whose anti-Nazi overtones are blatant; the book is published that fall. Promoted to the rank of captain, Jünger participates in the campaign in France, where he makes sure, above all, that civilians and monuments are spared.

1941   Appointed to the Paris general staff, which also includes his friend Speidel. Jünger keeps his journal, which informs us precisely about his social life and his encounters with Parisian writers and artists, as well as his readings of the Bible, which help him through the ordeal of being close to the Nazi horrors.

1941-42   He works on a text about *Peace*.

1942-43   In the winter, his friends on the major staff send him to the Caucasian front to sound out the reactions of officers to the possibility of a coup against Hitler.

1943   Death of his father.

1944   After Stauffenberg's abortive attempt to assassinate Hitler on 20 July, Jünger is induced to quit the army, and he retires to Kirchhorst. His son Ernst, released with great difficulty from prison, where he was incarcerated because of his opposition to Hitler, is sent to the front lines; he is killed on 29 November in the marble quarries of Carrara.

1945   *Peace* circulates surreptitiously. At the time of the final German debacle, Jünger is head of a local militia [*Volkssturm*]. After Germany's surrender, Jünger, despite his clear disavowal of Nazism, experiences the hostility of those who accused him of having been its precursor.

1948   He settles in Ravenburg.

1949   Meeting with Martin Heidegger. Jünger has experiences with drugs (cf: *Approches* (1970), *Heliopolis*).

1950   Relocation to Wilflingen, Swabia. Jünger moves into the house of the Great Forester, which belongs to the Stauffenberg family. Death of his mother. Jünger visits friends in Antibes. From 1965 to 1980, he gradually resumes his habit of going on long and frequent trips, which are described in volumes I and II of *Seventy Wanes* (1981). It would take us too long to detail them and, for that matter, the many literary prizes he has won.

1957   *The Glass Bees.*

1950   The start of the review *Antaios. The Wall of Time.*

1960   The death of Gretha Jünger. *The World State.*

1962   Marriage to Liselotte Lohrer, a trained archivist and author of academic writings.

1967   *Subtle Hunts,* which relates his experiences as an entomologist.

1977   Death of his favorite brother, Friedrich Georg. *Eumeswil.*

1979   Trip to Verdun. Peace medal of the city of Verdun.

1981   *Author and Authorship.*

1982   Jünger receives the Goethe Prize of the City of Frankfurt, which arouses vehement reactions among his adversaries.

1983   *Aladdin's Problem.*

1984   At Verdun, along with German chancellor Helmut Kohl and French president François Mitterrand, he participates in the tribute paid to the victims of both wars.

1985   *A Dangerous Encounter.*

1986   Travels to Malaysia and Sumatra. Receives the Bavarian Maximilian Order for Science and Art.

1987   *Twice Halley.* Receives the "Tevere" Literature Prize from president Cossiga of Italy.

1988   Travels to Paris with German chancelor Kohl and to the Seychelles islands.

1990   Prime minister Felipe Gonzales of Spain visits him in Wilflingen. Jünger visits the caves of Lascaux.

1993   On July 20, French president Mitterand and German chancelor Kohl visit him in Wilflingen. Death of his son, Alexander. Receives the Grand Prize "Punti Cardinali dell'Arte" during the Venice Biennale.

1994   The latest installment of his diaries, *Siebzig verveht IV,* is published.

1995   Jünger celebrates his 100th birthday.